NEW ZEALAND
by MOTORHOME

The kiwi, New Zealand's famous rare bird. (Photo by David Shore)

NEW ZEALAND
by MOTORHOME

David Shore and Patty Campbell

PELICAN PUBLISHING COMPANY
Gretna 1989

Library of Congress Cataloging-in-Publication Data
Shore, David, 1942-
    New Zealand by motorhome / by David Shore & Patty
Campbell.
        p.   cm.
    Includes index.
    ISBN 0-88289-716-0
    1. New Zealand—Description and travel—1981- —Guide-
books. 2. Van life—New Zealand. I. Campbell, Patricia
J. II. Title.
DU405.5.S48   1989
919.31'0437—dc19
                                            88-30307
                                                CIP

Information in this guidebook is based on authoritative data available at the time of printing. Prices and hours of operation of businesses listed are subject to change without notice. Readers are asked to take this into account when consulting this guide.

Manufactured in the United States of America
Published by Pelican Publishing Company, Inc.
1101 Monroe Street, Gretna, Louisiana 70053

To Colin Taylor,
who started it all

ACKNOWLEDGMENTS

Many people on both sides of the Pacific helped make this book possible. We owe our sincere thanks to:

Diane Anderson, Sjelden Boeltl, Bob Bynum, Kathleen Calhoun, Aisha Campbell, Mitzi Clark, Marion Fisher, Ken Goody, Ngaire Grieg, Malcolm and Margaret Johnson, Leighton and Shirley Jones, Brad Kembel, Maggie Kerrigan, Peter Manston, Nick Nicholson, Larry Rakow, David Ricquish, Anne Rykoski, Dean Shapiro, Bill Southward, Jack Street, Colin and Charmayne Taylor, Mike Turner, Thomas Wahlmann, Kim Wong, and all the people of the New Zealand Tourist and Publicity Department.

Contents

NEW ZEALAND
by MOTORHOME

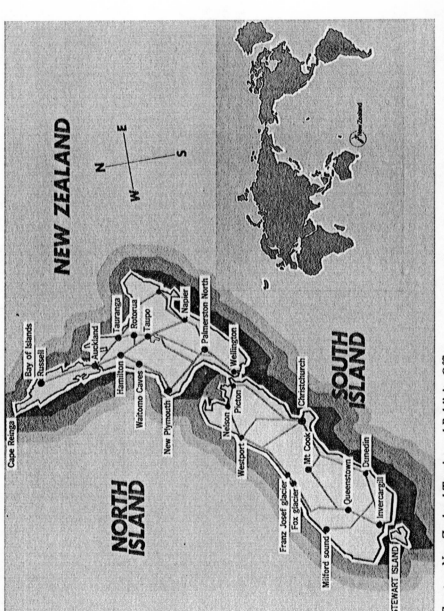

Courtesy New Zealand Tourist and Publicity Office

Introduction

AH, NEW ZEALAND!

Lazily lounging
in a natural
spring-fed
thermal pool,
soothed and tickled
by warm, silent bubbles,
a pair of tired
but happy
travelers
gaze up into
the velvety black night sky,
The Southern Cross glistens
like a great,
jeweled
pendant,
surrounded by more stars
than they've ever seen before . . .

as they reminisce
    dreamily
        about their experiences
here in the Land of the Long White Cloud.

They think about
    the fascinating walk through a warm,
                                lush
                                    fern forest,
        (no snakes in the grass)
        surrounded by
                    odd, friendly birds
                    weird, lacy ferns
                    and mast-straight, sky-high Kauri
                        trees.

They think about
    the glittering black sand beaches,
    the clear blue-green waters of the Tasman Sea,
    the long mystic curve of Ninety-Mile Beach,
        sacred to the Maori people,
    And of secluded lakeside lawns
        where they stopped to swim in water so clear
            they could see the trout swimming,
        and afterward a lazy picnic lunch of cheese
        and luscious tropical fruits.

They think about
    the magical sunshine,
            purer,
                brighter,
                    making colors glow,
                    and people smile.

        The clean breezes in constant pursuit of puffy
clouds

across the ever-changing Pacific
            sky
They remember the Volcanic Plateau
      where they peered into the chuckling throats
            of ancient geysers,
      smelled the sulphuric stink of the earth's innards,
      and walked at night among hissing ghost plumes
            of steam
      in the backyards
            of Rotorua.

They think about
      the Maori culture
            whose words are everywhere in the names on the
                  land.
      The ceremonies,
                  feasts,
                        and dances
      that tell the story of the arrival of the
            Maoris,
            paddling fierce-faced canoes all the long,
                  long,
                  miles from "Hawaiiki"
      to come at last to this beautiful place.

Then their thoughts drift
      to the South Island,
            remembering rolling through beautiful gorges,
            filled with glowing poplars,
                        whitewater rivers,
                        roaring waterfalls.

"How does all this vastness fit into one small country?"
      they asked each other.
And then they climbed aboard a ski plane
      and soared above the Southern Alps,

> *over gleaming Mount Cook,*
> *and landed on an ice-blue glacier.*

And last there was Milford Sound,
>*On the topmost deck of the boat,*
>>*bundled against the mist,*
>*they gazed open-mouthed as they glided past*
>>*glacier-carved cliffs,*
>>>*long, frothy waterfalls,*
>>>>*rock-basking seals,*
and dark mountains that rose close and sheer from the water,
>*squeezing the sky into a*
>>>*narrow*
>>>*ribbon*
>>>*of light*
>>>*overhead.*

After a while the backs of their necks ached from looking
>*up.*
>>>*But they kept on*
>>>>*anyway.*

Sighing happily, our adventurous couple reach for their towels and sit on the edge of the pool to cool off in the delicious night air. Their talk turns from the near-spiritual beauties of the landscape to the just plain fun they've had trying to take advantage of all the activities New Zealand has to offer. They have been swimming, surfing, diving, sailing, fishing, whitewater rafting, jet-boating, and cruising on an antique steamboat. On land they have tried hiking, skiing, mountain climbing, four-wheel drive safaris, horseback riding, golf, tennis, bicycling, and even cricket.

Talking of new friends, they think of the people—and the lack of them. In a land the size of Colorado, they have learned that there are only three million relaxed, smiling

"Kiwis"—handsome, very civilized folk, unhardened by population pressures. Our couple has noticed that the common greeting when passing on the street is a smile and a sideways tip of the head, as if to say, "Great life, isn't it?"

They remember observing that in New Zealand one doesn't feel culture shock so much as culture tingle—everything is familiar and easy to understand but just different enough to have an edge of the exotic.

They are grateful for the lack of hard-sell tourist hype. Almost nowhere did they see tacky souvenir schlock shops of the kind so plentiful in other parts of the world. Nor do people who work in the tourist industry develop that all-too-familiar calloused attitude. Everyone they've met has been especially warm and helpful.

They recall the farm stay they enjoyed, visiting overnight with a family and getting a first-hand look at life on a sheep station. They marvel again that New Zealand has 70 million sheep, outnumbering the people 23 to one. They remind each other to send a postcard soon to the sheepherding couple they had found so congenial.

Ah, but there's another glorious day ahead, a few kilometers up the road. Thoroughly relaxed now, they towel off and head for their motorhome, where their own cozy bed is always ready for them. They'll awake

> *when the warm New Zealand sun*
> *pierces the clear morning air*
> *and sets aglow the mist*
> *rising from the natural*
> *spring-fed*
> *thermal pool . . .*

WHY A MOTORHOME?

No other country is so perfectly suited to a motorhome holiday. The spectacular scenery, the lush forests, the breathtaking beaches, the interesting cities, the endless recreational opportunities, and the friendly people (not to mention the sheep) all draw you into a complete experience, much more than just sightseeing.

Renting or buying a motorhome or van for your New Zealand adventure gives you total freedom to explore wherever you choose in clean, civilized comfort, or to find a secret paradise and just relax.

You're free of the usual travel pressures. No checkout times, no packing and unpacking every day, no tour regimentation, no rushing to keep on schedule, no hotel bills, no tipping, and no restaurant bills (a big saving) unless you *choose* to eat out. You can eat fresher, more healthful foods. too. Many Kiwi vans and motorhomes are equipped with broilers so that you can enjoy the world's best lamb chops, fish, and beefsteaks for next to nothing.

Best of all, you get to meet the people; you can stop at roadside fruit stands, small-town "Hot Bread" shops, and those lovely Devonshire tea rooms for a real treat. You can stop at one of the beautiful rest areas for a picnic next to a lake, and find yourself fishing with a bunch of good-natured Kiwis. They're very relaxed and friendly people, and they all speak English. You're traveling as they do, not looking down at them from a tour bus, and you're accepted immediately. Friendships and priceless adventures bloom at every stop.

The driving experience itself is a pleasure. The roads are smooth, well-marked, and nearly empty. Most bridges are one lane; there's not enough traffic to warrant two. Kiwi drivers are courteous and forgiving.

And kids love it. Most motor camps have playground areas featuring trampolines, and there are plenty of other kids to play with. They can bring along their favorite toys, and they're spared the upset of strange food and strange beds. The motor camps, by the way, are the best we've seen. There are more than 400 of them in New Zealand, and every one we've visited is spotless, well-run, and full of happy people. And the showers are *always* hot.

Best of all, when there's not a single hotel room left in town, you've got a bed. And a kitchen, too.

A BIT OF GEOGRAPHY

New Zealand is made up of two long, narrow pieces of land called, logically enough, North Island and South Island. The total area is about the size of Colorado. Its recent volcanic origin is marked by the spine of sharp mountains that run down its length, and by several active volcanoes and many thermal areas. It lies isolated in the South Pacific, 1,000 miles southeast of Australia and 1,400 miles north of Antarctica. The largest city is Auckland, with a population of about a million. Next largest are Christchurch, on the South Island, and Wellington, the capital. The population is a little over three million, of which about 85 percent are of European origin, mostly British; 10 percent are Maori, and the rest are other Pacific Islanders and Asiatics. The principal industry (as any tourist can plainly see) is sheep-farming, but New Zealand is also the world's largest exporter of dairy products, and recently kiwi and other tropical fruits have become an important cash crop. The climate is generally cool and temperate, but phases into sub-tropical in the far north and sub-Antarctic in the far south, with frequent rain west of the mountains. The terrain is extremely varied, from the wild unexplored mountains of the southern tip, through rolling grasslands, native fern forest "exotic" cultivated pine forest, volcanic wastelands, and tropical beaches in the Northland.

A BIT OF HISTORY

According to Maori legend, New Zealand was fished out of the sea by the great god Maui. Until the arrival of humans there were no mammals, and birds evolved to fill their ecological niches, some species losing the power of flight and adapting to forage on the forest floor. This evolutionary trend culminated in the gigantic twelve-foot-tall moa, which was hunted to extinction by the earliest human inhabitants. During the last millenium, the Maoris arrived by canoe in successive waves from an unknown point of origin. The first European to visit New Zealand was the Dutchman, Abel Tasman, in 1642. He was prevented from landing by the fierce natives, but he nevertheless gave the country its name. Captain James Cook was the first European to set foot on New Zealand, when he circumnavigated it and claimed it for Britain In 1769. He was followed closely by the Frenchmen, Jean-François Marie de Surville and Marion du Fresne.

Rapacious exploitation by adventurers, traders, sealers, whalers, and missionaries soon grew to such a state that the British sovereign appointed a lieutenant-governor in the person of Captain William Hobson. Under his sponsorship the Treaty of Waitangi in 1840 gave the Maori chieftains the protection of the British Crown in exchange for the rights to much of their land. The resulting flood of farmers and settlers was more than the Maoris had bargained for, and in 1861 the decade-long Land Wars broke out in the north. Meanwhile, on the South Island, a Gold Rush had followed the discovery of the precious metal there.

During World War I and World War II, New Zealand suffered heavy losses and the pastoral economy was hard-hit by the Depression. Nevertheless, the country has developed a government distinguished by its humanitarian concern and a standard of living that in recent years has ranked among the world's highest.

CHAPTER 1

Making Pacific Plans
When To Go, What To Take, How To Do It

Now that you've decided you want to go to New Zealand and see it for yourself, it's time to come down from that puffy white cloud in the South Pacific sky for just a moment and deal with some nuts and bolts. There are a few tips we can give you to help you cut some red tape, save a little money, and have an easier, more enjoyable trip.

When To Go

Since the seasons are reversed in the southern hemisphere, you can flee a hostile winter and step into a warm, welcoming summer. But try to avoid Christmas vacation time, mid-December through January. That's the New Zealanders' favorite family holiday time, and it is peak tourist season as well. Everything is crowded, prices are highest, and the weather is hottest. You need reservations everywhere.

The best time to go is in February, March, and April. This is late summer/early autumn. It is the period of least rainfall, the weather is pleasant, and the roads are empty. The four-day Easter weekend is comparable to our Labor Day—the last big outing of summer—for the Kiwis, and things get crowded again. But it's tolerable, and it doesn't last long.

In April the weather begins to cool, but the ocean water off the North Island is still warm enough to swim. On the South Island, especially in the mountains, nighttime temperatures can get as low as freezing. But days are crisp and clear, the sun is warm, the trees have turned to gold, and the sandflies are mercifully scarce. If you prefer the glories of springtime, you'll want to see New Zealand between September and early December. There is a chance of a little more rain, but the country is absolutely gorgeous at that time. There are flowers everywhere, cute lambs in the fields, green green grass, and snow still on the mountains. Airfares are lower, too. This is also a "shoulder season" for airfares, with prices similar to the February-April period.

Booking Your Flight

The best in-flight food we've tasted was served aboard Air New Zealand 747s by a pleasant group of flight attendants. No plastic forks here; all passengers get real crockery and dinnerware and fresh New Zealand-grown food on the Government's own airline. It's the country's most visible showpiece, and the Kiwi touch is everywhere. Other airlines fly to New Zealand (Continental, Canadian Airlines International, Hawaiian, Qantas, United, and UTA), but ANZ is our favorite (and the only one with nonstop flights to Auckland *or* Christchurch).

Your travel agent can fill you in on current flights and fares, and make all the necessary bookings for you. To get more specific information (but not bookings), contact the New Zealand Tourist and Publicity Office (NZTP). (See "Information Sources" at the end of the book for the address and phone number of the NZTP office nearest you.)

It's a long flight—12 hours nonstop from Los Angeles—but if you have lots of time you can break it up with stops in Hawaii, Fiji, Tahiti, or Sydney, depending on the airline you choose. Different airlines have different restrictions on stopover time.

Speaking of stopovers, you may be treated to an un-scheduled one if your flight is delayed for your plane's crew to receive its legal amount of rest. You'll be put up in a hotel for four hours or so, then bused back to the plane. You won't have to go through the baggage-claim hassle on this stop-over, but you may wish to pack your toothbrush and what-ever else you'll need in your carry-on bag, just in case. And don't schedule too tightly on the other end, based on your projected arrival time.

Where to Land

You can choose to land in Auckland or Christchurch, de-pending on where you want to start your Kiwi adventure. There are advantages and disadvantages to each. Auckland is New Zealand's largest city, and the venue of many tourist attractions. It's also the best place to look for a van or motorhome to buy or rent, since it offers the largest selec-tion. If you want to see the North Island first, land in Auck-land.

Christchurch is the gateway to the South Island, and is also a large city with plenty of things to see and do. It too has a good selection of vans and motorhomes, but not as extensive as that in Auckland. If you want to start with the South Island, go to Christchurch.

Time Difference

New Zealand is just on the other side of the International Date Line from North America, and its time zone is 20 hours ahead of Pacific time. In other words, if you're on the West Coast of the U.S., right now in New Zealand it's tomorrow, four hours earlier. If you leave Los Angeles on Saturday evening, you'll arrive in New Zealand on Monday morning, having lost Sunday out over the Pacific. On the return trip you'll be home before you left. Daylight Saving Time, an advance of one hour, is in effect in New Zealand from the last Sunday in October to the first Sunday in March.

RED TAPE

Entry requirements are simple: You must have a passport that is valid beyond your expected stay in New Zealand; you must have a return or onward ticket; you must have sufficient funds to maintain yourself while in New Zealand; and you must be of good health and character. U.S. and Canadian citizens need no visa for visits of up to three months.

To stay longer, you must apply in person to the Department of Labour, Immigration Division, in either Auckland, Wellington, or Christchurch. There is no fee, and permission is usually issued on the spot. No vaccinations or health certificates are needed to enter the country.

Importation Restrictions

You may bring in goods of a combined value of up to NZ$500 free of duty and Goods and Services Tax (G.S.T.). You may bring in up to 200 cigarettes, 50 cigars or 250 grams of tobacco, or a combination of the three up to 250 grams. You may bring in up to 4.5 litres of wine or beer and one bottle of spirits or liqueur containing up to 1,125 ml.

Drugs

Of course, narcotic drugs are prohibited, but if you require prescription medicines containing them, you must have the prescription with you, and carry the drugs in their original containers.

Plants, Seeds, and Fruit

Importation of plants, seeds, and fruit is tightly restricted and strongly discouraged. A permit *and* an International Health Certificate are required, you must declare them, and they will be held for inspection.

Pets

Dogs, cats, and birds are not allowed, except for a few from Australia and the British Isles, with permits.

Food

You may bring in only coffee, tea, crackers, and cookies. They have plenty of the best of the latter three in New Zealand, but if you're a coffee lover, better bring your own.

Changing Money

In general, airports are not the best places to change currency. You will nearly always get a better exchange rate at a bank. Since you'll need some New Zealand money immediately upon arrival, we recommend changing about $100 at a bank at home before you leave. You can then put the rest of your money in travelers' checks (easily negotiable in New Zealand), or just rely on your VISA, Mastercard, or American Express card for drawing cash as you go. All are widely accepted there.

Don't convert all of your cash before you get to the airport. Both the U.S. and New Zealand charge a departure tax. In U.S. airports you'll pay an extra $18 per person; leaving New Zealand will cost you NZ$10 each.

WHAT TO TAKE

Since you're traveling by motorhome, we're not going to give you the traditional lecture about "traveling light." You won't have to. One of the more pleasant advantages of motorhome travel is that there's no need to pack and unpack every day. No more will you have to fold each thing just right, decide which suitcase to put it in and then remember it, sit on your luggage and try to tuck in all the loose ends just to get it closed, and lug it up and down hotel steps every day.

On this trip you'll need to pack only twice: when you leave home and when you leave New Zealand. Between those times you can relax and spread out and surround yourself with the things you choose. You're on vacation!

Clothes

Most vans and motorhomes have upright closets where you can hang dresses, sport coats, etc., but space is limited. Still, you won't need a lot of elaborate outfits, so it's best to keep it simple. Bring mostly soft clothes that you can fold into the variously-shaped storage compartments. Soft clothes are easiest to pack, as are soft suitcases, which fold up and stow out of the way.

A good clothes strategy for New Zealand involves two key words: "casual" and "layered." Because of the outdoor lifestyle, T-shirts, shorts, sweatshirts, and nice jeans fit in almost everywhere. The climate ranges from subtropical in the North to subantarctic in the South, and the temperature can vary widely in any one day. You'll want to bring both cool and warm clothes that will work together: a tank top that goes under a shirt that goes under a sweatshirt that can be topped with a vest and a windbreaker, for instance.

However, fine restaurants may have dress codes that re-.quire shirt and tie for men and skirts for women, and in Auckland and Wellington they dress with a great deal of elegance. You'll want to bring one nice outfit and the accessories that go with it.

Leave room in your luggage for one of the gorgeous hand-crafted sweaters you can buy in New Zealand. These are not only hand-knit, but often the same craftsperson raised the sheep, carded the wool, and dyed and spun the yarn. They're not cheap, but they'll look and feel great for a long time.

A startling sartorial feature of Kiwi life is the widespread wearing of shorts by men. We're talking solid color and moderate length here, not Hawaiian print mini-briefs. Even in the cities you'll see men in shorts with calf-length socks and regular shoes, For office wear they are sometimes combined with a dress shirt and tie, and a sport jacket if the weather is cool. According to Patty, the nationwide acceptance of this fashion has something to do with the fact that Kiwi men have extraordinarily good legs.

Clothes Packing Checklist

There are some items of clothing that we consider indispensable. You will surely have some additions and deletions, but this list will help you make sure you don't forget anything important:

—Well-fitting jeans or corduroy pants
—Permanent-press sport shirts and slacks (men)
—Permanent-press skirts (women)
—T-shirts and sweatshirts
—Warm sweater (or buy one there)
—Water-repellent windbreaker
—Light fold-up poncho or raincoat with hood
—Shorts (men and women)
—Cool tops for women
—swimsuits
—Comfortable walking shoes and sandals
—Plastic sandals (for showers and rocky beaches)
—Sport coat, white shirt, and tie (men)
—One nice skirt and top or dress (women)
—Dress shoes and socks or stockings

Motoring Needs

You will be driving a lot on this trip, so why not make the experience as pleasant and enjoyable as possible? There are a few items that you can take along to make your roads smoother (even the "unsealed" ones). They are little things that you don't normally consider necessary for your daily driving.

This is different. We hope you won't need some of these things, but you may be glad you have them along. You will probably want to personalize this list with some indispensable items of your own:

—Maps (see Chapter 3)
—Tool kit (basics for minor repairs)
—Aerosol tire inflator (just in case)
—Sunglasses (for the brilliant NZ sunshine)

—Binoculars (for reading street signs)
—Compass (helps you navigate)
—Convex mirror (for city driving; use on left side)
—Driving gloves (for cold mountain driving)
—Business cards
—Travel sewing kit
—Light nylon day pack
—Cameras and film
—240-volt adapter plugs (built-in in larger vans)
—Washcloths (not supplied with rentals)

And if you're planning to buy, not rent, your motorhome:

—Favorite wine glasses, coffee cups, dishes, silverware, etc.
—Towels and bedding

Papers

The papers, of course, are most important. You *can't* leave home without some of them, while others make it a lot easier. They are often difficult to replace, and often necessary. Check this list carefully before you leave for the airport:

—Passport
—Plane tickets
—Auto club card
—Credit cards (check expiration dates)
—Optical prescription
—Driver's license
—Travelers' checks
—Guidebooks

THE FLIGHT

The flight to New Zealand is not much different from any long flight over the ocean; there's lots of water and clouds to look at, and not much else. An overnight flight is best, as there is a period when the plane is darkened and most passengers go to sleep. If you can sleep on a plane, this nap will make the flight seem shorter and you'll arrive rested and less subject to jet lag. When you awake, you'll be greeted by a beautiful blue South Pacific sky, dotted with puffy white clouds and even rainbows. Shortly after a hearty Kiwi breakfast, you'll be landing in either Auckland or Christchurch.

Arrival

Upon arrival you'll go through baggage claim and customs. When you get to the airport's main concourse, look for the car rental booths and phones. If you've reserved a van or motorhome in advance, they'll be expecting you at the appropriate counter and your rig will be parked outside. If you haven't, you can pick up one of the courtesy phones and the company you choose will pick you up and take you to their rental facility nearby. But if it's a busy season, the model you want may not be available, or you may have to wait. It's better to book ahead.

THE FIRST DAY

No matter how much sleep you got on the plane, you'll feel a bit disoriented by the long flight and the unfamiliar surroundings. It's not a good time to get used to driving on the "wrong" side of a strange vehicle and keeping it on the "wrong" side of strange roads and streets. That will be easier to master tomorrow. Today it's much better to head straight for a motel and relax. Ask your travel agent, the NZTP, or your motorhome company to recommend one near the place where you will pick up your vehicle. Ask for one with a spa pool (hot tub) or spa bath (jacuzzi bathtub). It's absolutely the best cure for jet lag.

While you stretch out and relax after your hot soak, watching the TV news in your room will help you get used to the Kiwi accent. It will also give you a sense of what's happening in New Zealand and what's important to the people with whom you'll be talking and dealing. By the way, if you have trouble turning on the television, notice that electrical outlets on the wall have on-off switches.

Rest area near Whangarei. (Photo by David Shore)

CHAPTER 2

How to Get Rolling

Renting or Buying a Motorhome in New Zealand

Kiwis love to travel by motorhome (as evidenced by the great number of such vehicles rolling around other countries with "NZ" stickers on their tails), and they know it's the best way to enjoy their own beautiful land. So it comes as little surprise that, although tourism is increasing, nearly half the people buying and renting them are New Zealanders themselves.

This makes for a large, healthy, and well-organized industry, with a bewildering number of choices and considerations for your selection. There are rental vehicles available ranging from two to six beds, or berths, with a variety of chassis and interior designs. You can choose diesel or petrol (gasoline), manual or automatic transmission, power or "armstrong" steering. You can have color TV, thermostatic climate control, a microwave, a broiler, a shower, a toilet, and hot water from an electric-eye spigot. Some models have more cabinets than than a furniture store, while others require creative stowage skills. Rates vary widely from season to season. Some include insurance and G.S.T. (Goods and Services Tax); others do not, We'll lead you through this maze as best we can.

Then there is the purchase option. Dealers offer buy-back and sell-for-you arrangements, with guarantees of up to 75 percent return. Some offer a one-year mechanical warranty.

Rental companies sell vehicles from their fleets (but won't buy them back), and private sellers advertise in newspapers and magazines. More about all that later.

BYO (Bringing Your Own)

Unless you plan to stay in New Zealand for more than two months and you're very attached to your rig, it's not very practical to think about shipping it over there. You must take it home, too, and so you'll be paying for 14,000 miles of ocean travel. It's more expensive than other destinations because fewer ships go there.

For example, transporting a VW van will cost more than US$5,000 round-trip from Los Angeles, plus insurance and miscellaneous import fees, plus customs duty and the ever-present G.S.T. (refundable when you take it home). Shipping a 21-foot Winnie will cost upwards of US$13,000 round-trip. Any NZ vehicle that big would have a diesel engine, as petrol, even since deregulation, is not cheap.

Left-hand drive is another problem. Importation of such a vehicle is strictly forbidden. You can request a waiver for up to twelve months by writing the Ministry of Transport, Head Office, Private Bag, Wellington, at least three months in advance of your intended arrival. You must tell them the make, model, chassis number, and your dates of arrival and departure. Then you must be prepared to drive it on the left side of the road.

If you should decide to sell your vehicle in New Zealand, it must be converted to right-hand drive and you must pay sales tax. Also, your customs duty and G.S.T. will not be refunded. Not a good idea. The 1988 law was passed in response to people who brought vehicles from other countries to sell in New Zealand at a substantial profit, as well as other importers of left-hand drive vehicles, which are regarded as a safety hazard on New Zealand roads. Kiwi motorhomes are better suited to local conditions. *We do not recommend bringing your own.*

RENTING A MOTORHOME

If you have a month or less to spend in New Zealand, you'll be better off renting than buying. It's much quicker and easier, and the vehicle comes to you fully equipped, serviced, and ready to roll as soon as you are. The cost of repairs, if any, is reimbursed. Daily rates vary from NZ$60 to NZ$225, mileage included (most companies quote only daily rates). Price differences depend on the model you choose, the company and, most important, the season.

In fact, rates (and airfares) vary so widely from season to season (more than 200 percent in some cases), that you can save hundreds of dollars if you can adjust your travel dates to the rate changes. Dates of these changes are listed below with each company's brochure excerpt.

Booking in Advance

Most New Zealand motorhome rental companies get their bookings through "wholesalers," brokers of many different travel-related things. They are located in the U.S., Canada, the U.K., Europe, and other strategic places around the globe. These wholesalers make bookings of all types, and most deal only with travel agents, not with individual customers. Their reasoning on this is that individual customers take up their time with questions, while travel agents make most of the actual bookings.

Many travel agents can answer some of your questions about motorhomes, but they can't know all the specifics you're curious about. A few of the larger companies have toll-free telephone numbers for the public, and will speak to you and take your booking. They are:

Budget	(800) 472-3325
Hertz	(800) 654-3001
Mount Cook Line	(800) 468-2665

Contact information for these and other companies is listed with descriptions at the end of this chapter.

Choosing the Right One

There are lots of companies in New Zealand who would be glad to rent you a motorhome. Their rates are roughly comparable, as are the vehicles themselves.

Standard Equipment

One or more beds
Electric refrigerator
Gas cooker (stove)
Kitchen sink with water supply and pump
Kitchen counter space
Dining table
Cooking utensils
Crockery and cutlery
Food storage space
Linens and bedding
Portable electric heater
Radio (many with cassette player)
Standard automotive heater
Bucket for waste water

The Differences

However, that standard equipment can take many different forms. There are important variations from company to company in the floor plans and other design features which you should be aware of before you choose one over the others.

For instance, if you're six feet tall or more, you may be uncomfortable sleeping in most of the two-berth and 2 + 2 (two adults, two children) vans. Many people have told us they couldn't stretch out because there was a wall at either end of the bed, be it crosswise or lengthwise.

One exception is the Budget two-berth van; its lengthwise fold-out bed is open-ended and allows feet to hang over. The over-the-cab beds common to all of the larger motorhomes (and some smaller ones) are also a bit short for most adults, and climbing down and up those little vertical ladders in the middle of the night can be difficult. Those beds are good for kids (if they're old enough not to be in danger of falling out). They'll immediately clamber up there anyway.

High-top vans and 2 + 2s (like Maui's Mini) have extra storage space up top, but the added height makes them less stable in crosswinds and cuts fuel mileage. Pop-top vans offer the same headroom, but only when needed. And they're easy to "pop."

Most of the larger (four- and six-berth) motorhomes are based on Japanese diesel truck chassis, like Isuzu and Mitsubishi, while the smaller models favor the Toyota Hiace van and the Ford Courier pickup. Both of these have four-cylinder petrol engines. All are reliable and economical (22-24 MPG). The smaller ones drive like cars and allow higher cruising speeds (100 km/h or 62 mph) in comfort. The big diesels will hold you to 80 km/h or about 50 mph. They're noisier and rougher-riding.

Most vehicles have manual transmissions. If you're not used to shifting with your left hand, you might prefer an automatic. We have found this feature only on Budget vans. Most have linoleum-style vinyl floor coverings. If you prefer carpeting, you'll find it in Newmans and Mount Cook Line motorhomes. A built-in color television set comes with the Budget six-berth rig only.

All offer porta-potties, some charging extra for them, but none have holding tanks. For waste water, each comes with a plastic bucket to be placed under the drain pipe. All motor camps have dump sites for the buckets, and legislation to require holding tanks is in the process. Clean public facilities are easy to find in New Zealand, and the porta-potties are hardly ever needed.

In general, it's best to choose the smallest vehicle that you and your travel mate(s) will be comfortable with. Most of your time will be spent driving, and the smaller ones are more maneuverable, more comfortable, and easier to park (not to mention cheaper to rent). We are two average-size people, and we have tried them all, from a luxury six-berth to a two-berth pop-top. We prefer the latter.

Personal Requirements Checklist

You'll be a lot happier with your van or motorhome if you make sure these features meet your requirements:

- Is the vehicle less than two years old and/or in good condition?
  —Minor malfunctions can be major annoyances when you're on vacation.
- Is the engine diesel or petrol-powered?
  —Diesel is more economical, but noisier.
- Is the transmission manual or automatic?
  —Personal preference rules here.
- Does it have power steering and brakes?
  —Big rigs need them, smaller ones don't.
- Are the beds long enough and wide enough?
  —An important comfort consideration.
- Does it have a "griller" (broiler)?
  —Lamb chops and beef steaks are excellent and cheap here.
- Does the fridge switch automatically from 12V to 240V for hookups?
  —A big trouble-saver.
- Does it have an electric heater?
  —Nights can be nippy.
- Does it have toilet facilities?
  —Porta-potties are available; no holding tanks on NZ rigs.
- Is there adequate storage space?
  —This makes a big difference in comfort.
- Does it have a shower?
  —Needed only for freecamping; all motor camps have good ones.
- Do interior lights work without hookups?
  —Necessary for freecamping or emergencies.
- Is the driving position comfortable?
  —Seat, steering wheel, and pedals should feel good for long drives; check before accepting.
- Is there a good radio with cassette player?
  —Valuable for information and entertainment.
- Is adequate crockery, cutlery, linen and bedding provided?
  —Be sure there's enough for everybody in your party.

The charts and drawings at the end of this chapter should answer many of these questions. The information has been provided by the rental companies themselves.

MOTORHOME FEATURES AND RATES

To help you choose the best van or motorhome for your needs we've developed a standardized chart of important things to know about each one (see charts at the end of this chapter). You may use it for direct comparison. Two-berth models are available in either pop-top or high-top configurations; this is indicated on the left side of each chart. Abbreviations stand for beds, engine type (petrol or diesel), transmission (automatic or manual), expected fuel consumption (MPG), grill, oven, toilet, shower, hot water, length, and full low- and high-season rate, including insurance and G.S.T. in NZ$. Rates may vary. Extra cost options are shown, i.e., " + 10" means NZ$10 extra.

The address and telephone number of the head offices of each company is listed so that you may make direct contact if you wish. Your travel agent can handle your booking. No endorsement is expressed or implied.

BUYING A MOTORHOME

If you're planning to stay in New Zealand for more than a month, you may come out better financially if you buy a used campervan or motorhome and resell it when you're ready to leave. This is not as difficult or risky as you might think. It may look expensive, but that's due partly to the exchange rate and partly to the fact that prices are generally higher there. Remember, your selling price will be commensurate. It's the same market, buying and selling.

You can buy from a dealer or from a private owner. There are advantages and disadvantages to both. Dealers offer buy-back guarantees and mechanical warranties; private sellers offer lower prices. Depending on the season, you may be able to enjoy a motorhome holiday at little or no cost, or even make a profit. We'll tell you how and where to buy and sell wisely.

Private Sellers

Private owners advertise vans, motorhomes, and vehicles of all types in newspapers and magazines, and sell them at weekend car fairs and auctions. They are probably the least expensive source for buying a vehicle.

Making sure you get a good one is not difficult if you follow the procedures recommended under PROTECTIONS (later on in this chapter). Private sellers are usually easy to deal with, especially if they're desperate, and you could come away with a real bargain.

Classified Ads

A good place to begin your search is the *Auto Trader Magazine,* available at many newsstands. Like similar publications in the U.S., it features private party ads with pictures. These are especially helpful with the unfamiliar makes and models for sale in New Zealand. There are separate editions for the major cities, and a nationwide edition. Another good source of ads is the city newspaper. You'll find the most automotive classifieds on Wednesdays and Saturdays in the *New Zealand Herald* in Auckland, the *Press* in Christchurch and the *Dominion* in Wellington.

Car Fairs and Auctions

Private sellers come together on weekends to display their vehicles to prospective buyers. This gives you an opportunity to see them close-up, inside and out. You can compare them side by side and even drive them.

Newmarket Car Fair meets on Saturday mornings in the Auckland suburb of Onehunga, in the carpark at 164 Arthur Street. Vehicles priced at less than NZ$5,000 are shown from 8:00 to 9:30 A.M. Those asking NZ$5,000 to NZ$10,000 are shown from 9:30 to 11:10 A.M., after which come the high rollers, those priced above NZ$10,000.

Manukau and **Takapuna** car fairs meet on Sunday, and work similarly. They're also in suburban Auckland. All advertise in the *Herald* classifieds.

N.Z.M.C.A.

A very reliable and highly respected source is the New Zealand Motor Caravan Association (N.Z.M.C.A.). They list members' motorhomes for sale. Phone 462-744 or 490-370 in Auckland.

Dealers

The safest and easiest way to buy a used van or motorhome is through a dealer. It may cost a bit more, but you get some important extras that a private seller can't give you, not the least of which is peace of mind. Some of the major advantages are:

1. Guaranteed Buy-back. A very important consideration. You know at the outset that you can sell the vehicle on the day you plan to leave New Zealand, instead of spending a desperate week trying to unload it. *This is especially important if you will be leaving at or near the end of the tourist season, when everybody's selling and nobody's buying.* Here is where the higher purchase price pays off. You know exactly how much you will get back: 60 to 75 percent of your purchase price, agreed upon at the time of purchase and guaranteed in writing. But you don't have to sell your motorhome back to the same dealer; you are free to sell it to someone else if you choose.

2. Mechanical Guarantee. This is something you can almost never hope to get when buying from a private owner, who hopes never to see his van again. On the contrary, a firm who plans to buy the vehicle back has a genuine interest in its mechanical fitness. And since they are making sure it is fit, they can guarantee it. In order to do that, they must go through it, check everything out, and correct the deficiencies. That, of course, means you can logically expect to get a sound vehicle with no hidden surprises.

3. Repair Authorizations. A guarantee is worthless if the seller can't back it up. The dealer should be able to authorize repairs, if necessary, at professional facilities throughout the country, or be willing to reimburse you for repairs you must pay for yourself.

4. Reputation. Any business establishment is interested in maintaining a good name with satisfied customers. A good dealer will do what he can to make you happy. We've never met a dishonest or unfair Kiwi, but if you do, please let us know. We'd also like to hear of your good experiences with dealers. We'll include your evaluations in future editions.

Dealer Listing

The following is a list of dealers who sell campervans and motorhomes in Auckland and Christchurch, the two cities in which you're likely to be shopping. You may wish to contact them in advance of your trip to see what's available. Again, no endorsement is implied:

Auckland

Motor Home Centre, Ltd.
75 Great South Road, Otahuhu
Phone 276-3121 or 276-8837

Wood's Caravan & Motor Campers, Ltd.
83 Wairau Road, Takapuna
Phone 444-8131 or 444-6380

Endeavour Motor Homes
Phone 495-860

Mick Dagg Cars
279 Onehunga Rd., Onehunga
Phone 642-214

Garnet Motor Court, Ltd.
1096 Great North Rd., Pt. Chevalier
Phone 894-794

Hertz Car Sales
302 Great South Rd., Manurewa
Phone 267-3700

Christchurch

Cashel Car & Caravan Sales
342 Cashel Street
Phone 68-425

Hornby Caravan Centre
39 Carmen Road, Hornby
Phone 497-980

Don Hodges Caravans, Ltd.
207 Main South Road
Phone 483-706

Ted Youngman Caravans
49 Lincoln Road
Phone 384-659

Freedom Motorhomes
Phone 65-687

Gypsy Centre
48 Williams Road, Kaiapoi
Phone 27-6794

NOTE: your letter will get there faster if the suburban town name (*i.e.* Kaiapoi) is followed by the major city name (*i.e.* Christchurch). For example, the last address should read:

48 Williams Road, Kaiapoi
Christchurch, New Zealand

EVALUATING A USED MOTORHOME

When you've found a vehicle you like, whether it's in the hands of a dealer or a private owner, there are a few simple tests you can make. They will give you a fairly good idea of the condition of its vital parts. Run it through this checklist. If it passes all of these tests, it's probably a good buy:

1. Body Language. Think of your newly-met rig as a person. Tune in to its body language. Does it have a bright-eyed, eager look on its face? Does it stand straight and level on its wheels? If it has new paint, ask why. A vehicle less than 10 years old shouldn't require it except for custom bodywork or damage repairs. Look closely at the texture of the body surfaces. If it looks like it was molded out of putty, that may be the case. Look for file marks and lumps. Knock lightly with your fist all around the body and listen for changing sounds. A little bit of solid plastic filler sound is not bad; scratches and dents are a part of life. But if you find a lot of it, especially around door frames and other structural areas, this vehicle has been seriously hurt.

2. Rust. Check for excesive rust, particularly on a South Island vehicle. The rocker panels (below the doors) are usually the first parts to rust through. They're not as important as the frame and the floor pan, but they can tip you off to more critical problems underneath.

3. The Interior. Of course you'll want to check all the mechanical things thoroughly anyway, but starting with the interior lets you find out if you like being in the rig in the first place. That's the most important part, after all. You're going to be living in this thing for the whole time you're in New Zealand. Making you comfortable and happy is its primary responsibility. That's what separates it from all the impersonal, uncomfortable hotel rooms it will replace.

With that in mind, you can start checking out the livability of your prospective home on wheels. Pull down, set up, unfold, or do whatever is necessary to get the bed into sleeping trim. If it's a motorhome with permanent beds, that's good. If it's a van camper, the bed should be easy to work.

Look for a built-in two-burner stove with a detachable propane tank. These stoves are odorless and convenient, and light instantly. Propane refills are available all over New Zealand at motor camps, petrol stations and many stores.

An electric refrigerator is better than an icebox, of course. If the vehicle has one, it's a definite plus. Modern ones switch automatically from 12-volt battery power (while driving) to 230 volts (on motor camp hookups) to propane (for free-camping). Check for this feature.

A sink with water supply, pump and drain is a necessity, even if you don't plan to cook. It makes the difference between roughing it (with bottles of water) and being at home anywhere. Make sure the drain works well.

Check out the storage space. How efficiently is it used? Can you fit in all your gear and keep it organized in a convenient way? Vans and motorhomes vary a lot on this point, as do personal needs. Use your own judgment.

An AM-FM radio is nice to have, not only while driving, but in the evenings. New Zealand radio features comprehensive news, talk, and entertainment programming that will brighten up evenings in the motor camp. You'll want a cassette player, too, if you bring your favorite tapes from home.

4. Mechanicals. Once you're satisfied with the interior and general appearance of your candidate, it's time to see if it will be a trouble-free transportation device. After all, a major advantage of this mode of travel is being able to go and stop wherever *you* like, not where *it* decides.

Many vehicles in New Zealand are equipped to run on LPG (liquified petroleum gas) or CNG (compressed natural gas). These alternative fuels are cheaper than petrol or diesel, and are available throughout the country. It's a good feature to look for.

Here are the mechanical points you need to check carefully:

Starting

The engine should start easily when you turn the key. If you have to crank it a long time it may have been sitting for a while and there's no fuel in the carburetor. The seller should have started it before you came. Ruling out that condition, hard starting could indicate a weak battery, spark plugs needing replacement, valves needing adjustment or a valve job, or an engine needing a complete overhaul. You'll be able to feel that one (no power) when (if) it does start and you get rolling.

Brakes

Before you get rolling too fast, check the brakes. Just step on the pedal once and see if the vehicle stops. The pedal should be at least three inches off the floor. Step on it a few more times and see if it pumps up to a higher level. If so, keep your foot on it. If it slowly sinks down again, there is a leak or air in the system and the brakes are not to be trusted.

Feel

Does it feel good to drive? Don't compare it to your Cadillac back home, but look for smoothness, solidity, and ease of control. If this is your first experience driving a van or motorhome, it will feel strange, of course. Once you get used to it, though, you'll love it.

Does it have good power? Don't expect neck-snapping acceleration, but you'll feel it if it's strong and healthy. It will sound smooth, too. It should idle calmly and quietly and not threaten to die every time you stop at a traffic light. It should start up without stumbling.

Clutch

It should start up without shuddering, too. If the clutch doesn't engage smoothly, the pressure plate could be warped, the transmission mounts loose, or the flywheel about to fly off. The clutch pedal should not have more than two inches of play. Push it in with your hand to make sure. To really test the clutch, set the parking brake, put it in first gear and slowly let out the clutch. It should stall the engine and not slip. Do it just once; it's not good for the clutch. This test also tells you about the effectiveness of the parking brake.

Transmission

Run it up through the gears. Does it shift smoothly, easily, and solidly? Of course, you have to get used to the shift pattern, especially since you're shifting with your left hand. But if it's hard to get into gear after you've gotten used to it, there's a problem. It might mean worn synchronizers or worse. Test it for popping out of gear by going through all the gears, including reverse. Back it up and take your foot off the gas and see if it pops out. Try all the gears that way, accelerating up to about the speed where you would normally shift up, but don't. Just take your foot off the gas. In fourth gear, take it up to about 90 km/h. If it pops out of any gear when you lift your foot, the transmission is no good.

Engine Compression

We've already felt for the power and smoothness of the engine and listened for unseemly noises. Blue oil smoke from the exhaust is an indication of excessive wear that makes itself readily apparent. Now for the *real* engine test.

You should have a compression tester with you. If not, you can get one in New Zealand for less than NZ$20. It's a good investment. It will tell you if the engine is in good condition and will last out your trip without problems, or if it's about to expire. Blue oil smoke could indicate worn-out piston rings, but dirty oil can cause the same symptom. The compression test will tell you for sure.

Just pull out all the spark plugs, making sure you keep them in order so that you can put them back in the same cylinders. Look at the electrodes. Are they all the same color? They should be close. They should be beige or slightly darker, or even slightly grayish. If one or more is black and gooey, it is oil-fouled, indicating bad rings. The compression test will show that, too.

Hold the compression tester firmly in each spark plug hole (or screw it in, if you have that type), and hold it there while someone turns the ignition key, cranking the engine over six times or more. Check all the cylinders this way, writing down or remembering the readings. They should be within five pounds of each other. If they are all over 150 pounds, the engine is in good shape. With proper care it should give you a trouble-free tour of New Zealand. Readings slightly below

150, if uniform, are not too bad, but anything less indicates that this is an engine you don't want to depend on too heavily.

A van or motorhome that has gotten this far in the testing is doing well. We've considered all the important things—the ones that could stop you. This test is thorough enough for a permanent purchase, but for service like we are demanding from our machinery, it's good to know that everything is going to hold up. That's much more likely, of course, if you take it easy. Drive gently and it will treat you right.

Protections

If you'd rather not deal with the mechanical parts of the preceding evaluation test, you can have your proposed purchase inspected for you for about NZ$50. The Automobile Association (AA) has a program whereby they will do the evaluating and tell you everything it needs. They will then recommend a mechanic who can tell you how much each item of repair will cost. You may then use that information as a bargaining tool. This service is available to members of reciprocal automobile clubs in other countries (i.e. the AAA or NAC in the U.S.).

Two or three days' notice is normally required for this service, or it can be prearranged for a certain date by writing to the AA office in the appropriate city.

Addresses:

Automobile Association
33 Wyndham Street
P.O. Box 5
Auckland, New Zealand

Automobile Association
342 Lambton Quay
P.O. Box 1053
Wellington, New Zealand

Automobile Association
210 Hereford Street
P.O. Box 994
Christchurch, New Zealand

Running the vehicle briefly through the do-it-yourself evaluation test will tell you if it's worth the trouble and expense of the mechanic's inspection. It's not really as complicated as it looks on paper.

If you are not a member of an AA-reciprocal automobile club, you can do the same thing with an independent mechanic. It will probably cost you more, however.

The following is a checklist of official documents and legal requirements necessary to operate a motor vehicle in New Zealand:

Warrant of Fitness

To operate on New Zealand's roads, every motor vehicle must have a current Warrant of Fitness (WOF). This is a sticker displayed on the right side of the windshield. It certifies that the vehicle has recently passed a safety inspection and the brakes, steering, lights, and other parts necessary for safe operation are in working order. It also certifies that its structural integrity is not impaired by rust-through, and its exhaust emissions are within legal limits.

The WOF must be renewed every six months if the vehicle is more than three years old, and once a year if it is newer. When it is sold the WOF must be valid for at least five months. NOTE: a valid WOF assures you that the vehicle is safe, but not necessarily that it's a good buy. It says nothing about the condition of the engine, transmission, or other drive train parts.

Registration

When everything has been checked out and you've made your best deal, the paperwork is easy. The seller should sign the Ownership Certificate, releasing his or her interest in the vehicle. This document is important; it contains the names and addresses of all the owners the vehicle has had since it was new.

You then must take the Ownership Certificate to the nearest post office for a registration change. The cost is NZ$56, payable by the seller. The Annual Renewal Fee is a separate thing; it must be paid every June for every vehicle. If it is coming due soon, it should be figured in the deal.

Insurance

Motor vehicle insurance is compulsory in New Zealand, and it's not overly expensive if you know where to go. You can get impartial information and advice through the Insurance Inquiry Service, Insurance Council of New Zealand, P.O. Box 586, Christchurch. The phone number is (03) 798-950.

For the specific needs of motorhomers, the best source we've found is the New Zealand Motor Caravan Association (N.Z.M.C.A.), a voluntary organization dedicated to "the fostering of the self-propelled caravan movement." Its purpose is to benefit all motorhoming activity throughout the country, which includes arranging "the best coverage available today at the lowest cost."

To this end they will sell you a policy specifically designed for full coverage of a motorhome and its equipment and contents, as well as third party liability of up to NZ$1,000,000. As a special service, they offer an annual premium for overseas visitors of NZ$200 for the first NZ$3,000 value, plus NZ$15 for each additional NZ$1,000 value. For three or six months' insurance, divide this by 4 or 2, respectively. Add NZ$27.50 for the Visitor Membership Fee.

Contact E.M. Zimmermann, Planning and Insurance Officer, New Zealand Motor Caravan Association, Inc., P.O. Box 31-261, Milford, Auckland 9. Phone 462-744 or 499-458.

Now that you've got your home on wheels and everything is legal and proper, it's time for fun. Stow your gear and get rolling. New Zealand awaits!

HOLIDAY TOURS
30 Battersea Street
Christchurch
Phone 798-485

Beds	Eng	Tran	MPG	Grl	Oven	Tlet	Shwr	HtWtr	Lgth	Full Rate
2+1	P	M	25						15'	65 – 149
2+2	P	M	25						17'	70 – 154
4	D	M	20						17'	76 – 167

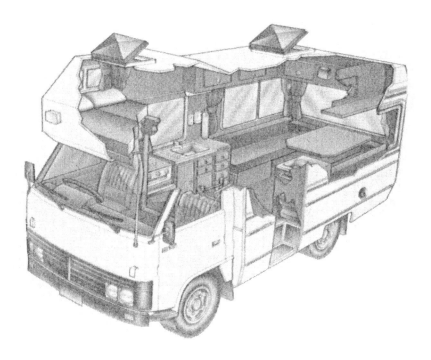

HOLIDAY TOURS 4 PLUS 2 MAXI/CRUISER

ENDEAVOUR MOTORHOMES
39 Rennie Drive
Auckland Int'l Airport, Mangere
Auckland
Phone 275-3034

	Beds	Eng	Tran	MPG	Grl	Oven	Tlet	Shwr	HtWtr	Lgth	Full Rate
POP	2	P	M	28			+10			15'	63 - 141
	4	D	M	28			+10			17'	74 - 174
	6	D	M	20							96 - 207

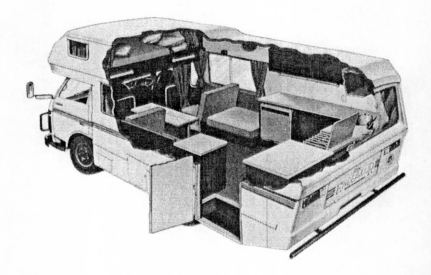

ENDEAVOUR 4/5 BERTH

HERTZ MOTORHOMES
44-46 Lichfield Street
Christchurch
Phone 60-549

	Beds	Eng	Tran	MPG	Grl	Oven	Tlet	Shwr	HtWtr	Lgth	Full Rate
HI	2	P	M	26	Yes					15'	88 - 154
	4	D	M	26	Yes					17'	99 - 193

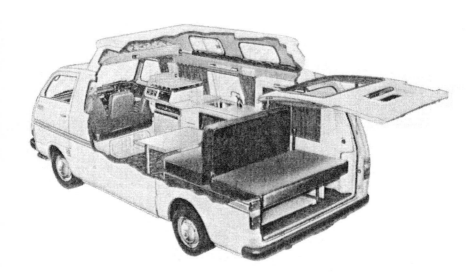

HERTZ 2 BERTH

BUDGET MOTORHOMES
P.O. Box 73-126
Auckland Int'l Airport, Mangere
Auckland
Phone 275-6672

	Beds	Eng	Tran	MPG	Grl	Oven	Tlet	Shwr	HtWtr	Lgth	Full Rate
POP	2	P	A,M	28	Yes					15'	
	4/6	D	M	28	Yes	Yes	Yes			19'	
	6	D	M	22	Yes	Yes	Yes	Yes	Yes	21'	

BUDGET EXECUTIVE EXPRESS

NEWMANS MOTORHOMES
P.O. Box 22-413, Otahuhu
Auckland
275-0709

	Beds	Eng	Tran	MPG	Grl	Oven	Tlet	Shwr	HtWtr	Lgth	Full Rate
POP	2	P	M	23	Yes					16'	72 - 145
	2+2	P	M	22	Yes					16'	77 - 174
	4	D	M	26	Yes		Yes			16'	86 - 200
	6	D	M	22	Yes	Yes	Yes	Yes	Yes	23'	111 - 239

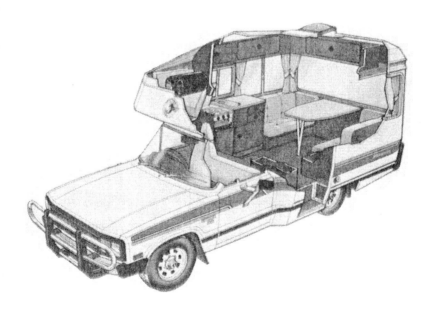

NEWMANS 2 PLUS 2 CAMPERVAN

New Zealand "traffic"--a sheep drive near the Southern Alps. (Photo by David Shore

BLUE SKY MOTORHOMES
41 Veronica Street, New Lynn
Auckland 7
Phone 876-399

	Beds	Eng	Tran	MPG	Grl	Oven	Tlet	Shwr	HtWtr	Lgth	Full Rate
HI	2+1	P	M	28	Yes					16'	
	4	D	M	28	Yes				Yes	17'	
	6	D	M	20	Yes		Yes	Yes	Yes	17'	

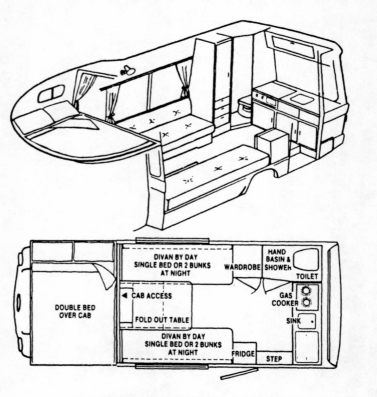

BLUE SKY SERIES 2600

ADVENTURE VANS
142 Robertson Road, Mangere
Auckland
Phone 275-8994

	Beds	Eng	Tran	MPG	Grl	Oven	Tlet	Shwr	HtWtr	Lgth	Full Rate
POP	2	P	M	28	Yes		+10			14'	64 - 141
	2+2	P	M	28			+10			15'	69 - 157
	4+2	D	M	28			+10			15'	75 - 174
	6	D	M	20		Yes	Yes	Yes		21'	97 - 218

HORIZON HOLIDAYS
530 Memorial Avenue
Christchurch
Phone 535-600

	Beds	Eng	Tran	MPG	Grl	Oven	Tlet	Shwr	HtWtr	Lgth	Full Rate
POP	2	P	M	25	Yes					15'	82 - 145
HI	2+1	P	M	25	Yes					15'	82 - 145
	2+2	P	M	22	Yes					16'	86 - 150
	4	D	M	26	Yes		Yes			16'	96 - 183
TWIN	4-2	D	M	20	Yes	Yes	Yes	Yes	Yes	20'	128 - 194
CAB	6	D	M	22	Yes	Yes	Yes	Yes	Yes	22'	130 - 217

MAUI CAMPAS
100 New North Road
Auckland
Phone 793-277

	Beds	Eng	Tran	MPG	Grl	Oven	Tlet	Shwr	HtWtr	Lgth	Full Rate
HI	2	P	M	25	Yes	+1.50				14'	66 - 140
	2+2	P	M	22	Yes	+1.50				13'	72 - 168
	4	D	M	22	Yes	+1.50				16'	80 - 195
	6	D	M	20	Yes	Yes	Yes	Yes	Yes	19'	106 - 23

MOUNT COOK LINE
47 Riccarton Road
Christchurch
Phone 482-099

	Beds	Eng	Tran	MPG	Grl	Oven	Tlet	Shwr	HtWtr	Lgth	Full Rate
HI	2	P	M	25	Yes					14'	64 - 143
	4+2	D	M	22	Yes		Yes	Yes	Yes	16'	103 - 21
	6	D	M	20	Yes	Yes	Yes	Yes	Yes	19'	

CHAPTER 3

Roads and Driving

Judder Bars, Roundabouts, and One-Lane Bridges

Driving in New Zealand is like that daydream that comes to you when you're stuck in rush-hour traffic, surrounded by honking horns, choking fumes, and frustrated drivers swearing at each other.

It's just the opposite here. You sail along smooth two-lane blacktop roads gently winding through bucolic scenery, with so little traffic that one-lane bridges are sufficient, and relaxed, cooperative drivers who smile and wave as you pass.

KEEP LEFT

Of course, nothing is perfect. As sure as Christmas comes in midsummer and water swirls counterclockwise down the drain, they drive on the left side of the road "down under." Your van or motorhome will have its steering wheel on the right-hand side and you'll be shifting with your left (the accelerator, brake, and clutch pedals are arranged the same as on U.S. models, however). The prospect can be scary, but in practice it takes only a short time to get used to it.

At first you must be very alert and conscious of the new orientation until habit patterns set in. With that in mind, try

Campervan overlooking Marlborough Sounds. (Photo by David Shore)

to drive as little as possible on that first jet-lagged day. After a day or so of carefully staying left, you'll find that your reflexes will take over nicely. However, it's important to be aware of times when you might be vulnerable to reverting unconsciously to your old ways.

Out in the country you can drive for miles without seeing another vehicle to remind you which side of the road to be on. It's easy to stray over to the right side then, or while you're overwhelmed by the scenery, or when you're tired or distracted. Establish a mental image of the driver next to the centerline, Just like at home. The navigator can help, too, by calling out "LEFT" whenever the driver seems to forget.

Right Turns

A right turn here is the tricky one, like a left turn at home. It's important to remember to look to the *right* on right turns, as you must cross traffic coming from that direction as well as oncoming traffic. The navigator can help in this case, too, by always watching for traffic coming from the left (often a blind spot for a motorhome driver) and saying "OK Left" if it's safe to pull out.

The "Keep Left" orientation applies also to foot traffic on city sidewalks. People there tend to pass each other on the left, and you may find yourself drifting and bumping at first.

What's more important is to look to the *right* first before you cross a street. Hitchhikers, by the way, stick out their left thumbs.

THE ROADS

New Zealand's roads are among the best in the world, in most places. Except for a few kilometres of multi-lane motor-way around the major cities, they're all two-lane macadam, very well-maintained and signed. You'll see few billboards and almost no litter to desecrate the scenery. An extra lane is often provided for slow traffic on long uphill stretches, but in general passing is no problem since there are usually not

A car yields the right of way at a one-lane bridge. (Photo by David Shore)

many oncoming cars to deal with. There are plenty of "lay-bys," places to pull off the road and rest or look at the scenery. Mountainous terrain sometimes necessitates tight curves, but they just make driving more interesting.

Unsealed Roads

Some of the roads are not "sealed," or paved, quite yet. They are few, however, and their numbers are dwindling rapidly. Even they are usually well-graded and fairly smooth, although you may encounter a washboard surface in a few places. Notable among those few places are the Coromandel Peninsula, the Milford Road, and the Haast Pass.

There are two kinds of unsealed roads. The better ones are called "metalled" roads. The "metal" is actually crushed rock spread over a dirt road, but not stuck down with tar. It must be renewed periodically. Some roads have no "metal," or it's all worn away. They are just dirt roads.

The dirt roads are dusty, so it's a good idea to close your windows while driving on them. If it's hot, you can open the fresh-air vents, which take in the un-dusty air ahead of the front wheels. If you encounter an oncoming car, close the vents until the air clears. Beep your horn when approaching blind curves; without a centerline drivers could forget to keep left. And keep your speed down even though the road seems smooth; bumps and potholes can appear suddenly.

Restricted Roads

Many rental companies will ask you not to drive their vehicle on certain roads because of difficult or dangerous conditions. At first you may scoff and say, "I can handle any road," but they may know a bit more about their own country than you do.

For instance, we met a man who had seen cars and buses driving safely on Ninety Mile Beach and decided his rental company was being overly cautious in asking him not to. He tried it and got stuck. Twice! He had to hire two bulldozers to pull him out.

Another couple we knew wanted to drive down the road to Milford Sound instead of taking the sightseeing bus. They did not run off the road while looking at the scenery, as many do (six cars a day in high season), but they did suffer *two* flat tires on the rocky surface, with only one spare. They had to change both tires in the rain after waiting for another van of the same size and from the same company to come along, flagging them down, and somehow borrowing *their* spare to get them into town. They then had no time for their boat tour of Milford Sound, one of the major highlights of a New Zealand holiday. We recommend you heed the warnings about restricted roads, or send us *your* horror story for the next edition.

Signing

Outside of the cities the roads are well-marked, although the signs don't give you much advance warning of crossroads or alternate routes. Keeping one jump ahead on the map and making decisions in advance will prevent crossroads confusion and fork-in-the-road fumbling.

To our eyes, accustomed to giant superhighway direction boards, the signing seemed inconspicuous and easily overlooked until we caught on. Then we began to appreciate the little yellow arrow-shaped signs which direct one not only to towns, streets, and motor camps, but also to geographic features, churches, points of interest, public buildings, and toilets. They are called "fingerboards," and they're provided by the Automobile Association. Each bears the AA logo. But in the cities, the signs are just as small and inconspicuous, even though they have many other signs to compete with. This makes it more of a challenge to find your way around, or to find the motorway out. A pair of binoculars will help you read the tiny signs across the intersections.

One-Lane Bridges

A shock to the first-time visitor to New Zealand is the phenomenon of the one-lane bridge. "What a crazy idea!"

you might say. "They must cause traffic jams, right-of-way fights, and accidents!" Well, they don't. In fact, traffic is so light out in the country, there's rarely another vehicle in sight when you come upon one.

Here's how it will look:

Your first warning is a diamond-shaped sign that says simply "ONE LANE BRIDGE." When you arrive at the bridge, you'll see another one. It may have a rectangular sign below it saying "PLEASE GIVE WAY." If so, you must yield the right of way to any oncoming vehicle. If not, that sign is on the other side of the bridge, and any oncoming vehicles must give way to you.

Roundabouts

These things are supposed to keep traffic moving, but drivers new to them may find them a bit disconcerting. Roundabouts are those circular intersections where everyone has to join a revolving flow, whether they want to turn or go straight. Then they must find the appropriate road and turn onto it. It's easy to miss your turn and go flying off in the wrong direction.

Here's how to get through a roundabout safely and pointed the right way:

When approaching the roundabout you need not stop, but you must give way to vehicles coming around from the right. When it's clear, you pull out, turning left (never right) to join the clockwise flow. It's best to stay on the outer edge of this merry-go-round, so that you can jump off safely when you suddenly find that you've come around to the road you want to be on.

The navigator must figure out which road to turn onto and tell the driver, who is busy avoiding other vehicles. Driving and reading directional signs is a two-person job in a strange situation like this. Fortunately, Kiwi drivers are courteous, cooperative and non-competitive, and will usually give you a wide berth.

If you miss your turn, no problem. Just go around again and catch it next time.

Rest Areas and Scenic Points

New Zealand's highways are blessed with a good supply of pleasant roadside rest stops, many in scenic locations. Most are nicely landscaped, with shade trees and picnic tables, while others are just places to pull off the road. Many are located next to a lake or forest, with hiking trails leading off into the bush. Very few have toilets, but the government has promised more in the future.

They're easy to spot: look for a square yellow sign that reads "REST AREA 400 M." Start slowing down, and 400 meters down the road you will see another yellow sign, about the same size but arrow-shaped on one side. It will say simply "REST AREA," and point to it. It's usually on the left side of the road.

Scenic Points are places where you can pull off the road and look at the view. They're just like scenic overlooks in the U.S., and are marked with signs like those marking rest areas.

Finding Fuel

Keeping your fuel needle above empty is not difficult in New Zealand. Except for a few long stretches of wilderness road, you're usually not far from a town with at least one station pumping petrol and diesel. LPG (liquified petroleum gas) and CNG (compressed natural gas) are found less often, although both fuels are gaining popularity and becoming more widely available. If your vehicle uses one of these fuels, you should have a listing of places to get it.

Most stations give "full service," which means that they handle the pump and often wash the windscreen (windshield). You must check your own oil and tires. Petrol and diesel prices vary from station to station, so it pays to shop around.

Credit Cards

The oil company credit card you use at home will not work at that company's stations in New Zealand. Most stations will, however, accept Mastercard, VISA, and sometimes other major cards. If you use one, don't sit and wait for the attendant to bring the bill out to you for signature. He or she is waiting for you to come inside and sign it at the register. Don't get annoyed; it's just the way it's done there. No extra charge is made for credit card use. The form and the procedure are the same as in the U.S., and the purchase is added to your bill like any other.

RULES OF THE ROAD

Traffic laws in New Zealand are similar to those in most civilized countries, and common sense will keep you out of trouble in most cases. A copy of the *Road Code* is available from any AA or NZTP office. There are few differences from U.S. driving laws. The important ones are:

Speed Limits

Open road: 100 km/h (vehicles over 3,000 kg: 90 km/h)
Cities and towns: 50 km/h

Seat Belts

Must be worn by all passengers. Small children (under 15) may not ride up front without child seats or restraints.

School Buses

May be passed when stopped, even when letting children on or off. Speed must not exceed 20 km/h.

Traffic Police

The local police cars you will see in cities and towns are painted various colors, but all are marked "POLICE." The officers driving them are usually friendly and helpful, and they are not concerned with your driving. That's the domain of the Traffic Police. They drive black and white cars that look like small California Highway Patrol cars, with similar radar guns sticking out the windows. These officers *are* concerned with your driving, especially your speed. You may wish to keep an eye out for them on the highway. They are usually found near towns.

GLOSSARY OF DRIVING TERMS

It's the same language, but Kiwis have a slightly different way of saying some things. You may see signs on the road that you don't understand, even though they're written in what looks like plain English. They're important. Here are the signs you'll see most, and what they mean:

Change down. Shift to lower gear.

Compulsory stop. Stop sign.

Concealed entry. Blind intersection.

Free turn. OK to turn on red light.

Give way. Yield right of way.

Judder bars. Speed bumps.

LSZ (Limited Speed Zone). 50 km/h when children are present or other conditions warrant extra caution; otherwise 100 km/h.

New seal. Loose gravel after road work.

Seal ends. Pavement ends here.

Slips. Falling rock.

Subway. Underpass.

Panel beaters. Body shop. (Not to be confused with *body shop* which is a massage parlor.)

Metres, Litres, and Kilometres

That's meters and liters in American. New Zealand has been on the metric system since 1980, when it began a complete changeover to more efficiently deal with other trading nations. That means you can't buy a gallon of gas or go a mile down the road.

Petrol is sold by the litre (l), which is 1.057 quarts. A U.S. gallon equals 3.785 litres. For convenience, just figure about four litres to the gallon.

Distances are expressed in kilometres (km), one of which

equals .62 miles. Therefore, the national speed limit of 100 km/h translates to 62 mph in our terms, and 50 km/h equal 31 mph. The popular advance-warning distance of 400 metres is just about a quarter of a mile.

To compute your motorhome's gas mi—er, sorry—*fuel consumption,* divide the number of km traveled since the last fillup (the trip odometer is handy for this) by the number of litres of fuel used. This should give you a figure like 8 km per litre (about 23 mpg). If you want a more accurate mpg figure, divide the km by .62 to get the miles traveled, and divide the litres by 3.785 to arrive at the gallons used. Then just divide the miles by the gallons for the mpg.

Comfort Stops

Every traveler needs a place to stop and go once in a while. Fortunately, this is not a problem in New Zealand. Most petrol stations and sit-down restaurants have clean, modern facilities, and the proprietors never ask if you're a paying customer even if you have to request the key.

They don't mince words there, either; if you ask for a restroom or a bathroom, you'll be referred to a place to rest or bathe. In polite Kiwi company, the word is toilet. If you Just can't bring yourself to say that, ask for the "loo," or look around for the two doors labeled "Ladies" and "Gents."

Nearly every town along the road will have a Plunket Room, a small house maintained by the Plunket Society to safeguard the health of mothers and preschool children. Each one is kept spotless and contains a sort of well-baby clinic and a Ladies room (but no Gents). There is often a pediatric nurse on duty. The facilities are free.

MAPS AND GUIDEBOOKS

Good maps and at least one sound guidebook are essential for a quality trip. You'll need, first, an overall map of the country for preliminary planning. "Introducing New Zealand," which is available free from the NZTP, packs a surprising amount of information into a convenient size. It includes a good planning map.

On the road you'll need more detailed maps. We like the *Shell Road Maps of New Zealand,* which binds regional and city maps (but no overall map) into one 9″ × 11″ book. It saves a lot of shuffling and folding. More detailed local maps can be picked up free at AA offices as you go.

The most detailed guidebook we've seen is the *Mobil New Zealand Travel Guide* by Diana and Jeremy Pope (Reed Methuen). It comes in two long, narrow volumes, *North Island* and *South Island,* and is breathtakingly thorough in its information about history and geography, as well as the most minute details about local sightseeing. For each town it gives a list of "Things to see and do," rated by interest, and for larger towns there are "Suggested drives" around the nearby countryside.

There is a wealth of other helpful books about New Zealand, many with stunning color photos. For a list of titles and information on where to get them, see "Where to Find Out More" at the end of this book.

ACCIDENTS

If you are involved in a road accident in New Zealand, the procedure is very much the same as at home. The police must be notified within 24 hours (48 hours if the owner of the other vehicle is not present). You must give whatever assistance is possible to anyone who has been injured.

A comforting twist is New Zealand's policy of providing free medical care to anyone, citizen or visitor, who has been injured in an accident. Regardless of fault, victims are compensated for reasonable expenses directly resulting from the accident, such as hospital and other medical expenses. Also provided are lump sum payments for permanent incapacity and certain other conditions resulting from the accident.

HELP ON THE ROAD

If you're a member of the American Automobile Association (AAA), the National Automobile Club (NAC), or one of the major Canadian automobile clubs, you're in luck. These clubs have reciprocal agreements with the New Zealand Automobile Association (AA), and you are entitled to full membership privileges. Included are emergency road service, maps and routing assistance, pamphlets, legal help, etc; generally the same benefits you get from your home club. Here is a listing of the 13 regional offices of the AA:

Auckland
33 Wyndham Street, Auckland
Tel. (09) 774-660

Canterbury
210 Hereford Street, Christchurch
Tel. (03) 791-280

Central
342 Lambton Quay, Wellington
Tel. (04) 738-738

Marlborough
23 Maxwell Road, Blenheim
Tel. (057) 83-399

Nelson
45 Halifax Street, Nelson
Tel. (054) 88-339

North Otago
273 Thames Street, Oamaru
Tel. (0297) 49-105

Otago
450 Moray Place, Dunedin
Tel. (024) 775-945

South Canterbury
Cor. Church & Bank streets, Timaru
Tel. (056) 84-189

Southland
47-51 Gala Street, Invercargill
Tel. (021) 89-033

South Taranaki
121 Princes Street, Hawera
Tel. (062) 85-095

Taranaki
49 Powderham Street, New Plymouth
Tel. (067) 75-646

Wairarapa
Cor. Chapel and Jackson streets, Masterton
Tel. (059) 82-222

Wanganui
78 Victoria Avenue, Wanganui
Tel. (064) 54-578

CHAPTER 4

Sleeping in the Best Places

Now that you're on the road with your new motorhome, where are you going to stay when it gets dark? Like everything else in New Zealand, finding a place to spend the night is comfortable and easy. Excellent campgrounds are everywhere and they are always clean and pleasant. New Zealand has the best motor camps that we have seen in all our years of campervan travel in Europe and the U.S.

But the orientation is different from the American idea of what camping is all about, and this takes some explanation. In the U.S.A., when we go camping, in the back of our heads is some sort of idea of returning to our pioneer heritage. We like to go off in the wilds (or pretend we're off in the wilds) and build a bonfire for roasting hot dogs and marshmallows. We like to scare ourselves at night with stories of bears and snakes, and we like to think that we're roughing it. Consequently our campgrounds tend to be way off in the wilderness and the individual camp sites as widely separated as possible to give the illusion of solitude.

In New Zealand campgrounds are called "motor camps" or "caravan parks" or "holiday parks." They are convenient, comfortable places to spend the night inexpensively, not wild

71

DeBrett's Thermal Valley Motor Camp. (Photo by David Shore)

Motor camp community kitchen. (Photo by David Shore)

retreats. The grounds are nicely landscaped with grass and flowers and trees, but wilderness it's not. You may be closer to your neighbors than you're used to, and open fires are *never* allowed. There will probably not be picnic tables and certainly not firepits (although there may be barbeque braziers). But there *will* be a wide range of civilized comforts to make your stay pleasant.

How to Find a Motor Camp

Those who like to plan ahead will want to make use of the Directory of Motor Camps at the end of this chapter, A more detailed list can be found in the pamphlet titled "Camp, Cabin & Caravan Accommodation—Guide to New Zealand Holiday Parks." The rental company will tuck a copy in the glove compartment of your motorhome, or you can get it from the New Zealand tourist offices, either before you leave home or when you arrive in NZ. However, except in unusual circumstances, you really won't need it. Every hamlet will have at least one camp, and large towns and resorts will have several. To find your haven for the night simply drive into a town and follow the yellow arrow signs marked "motor camp" or "caravan park." At the peak holiday period of late December to mid-January you might want to phone a couple of days ahead to make reservations at major tourist resorts. At any other time you should have no problem if you just arrive. The only two places where you might anticipate any difficulty in locating a campground are Auckland and Wellington. See Chapter 10 for directions to motor camps in these cities.

Campground Procedure

As you enter the grounds, there will be signs directing you to the office. Park before you proceed any further and go in and register. Unlike European camp managers, Kiwis never ask for your passport or hold it hostage. Charges are per person regardless of the size of your vehicle, and electrical hookups (called "power points") are included. The usual price range is NZ$12-14. You are expected to pay for your entire stay in advance (which makes getting away in the morning much simpler), and Visa and Mastercard are usually accepted. Your host will invariably be warmly welcoming and will often take time to show you around the grounds proudly. Sometimes you will be assigned to a numbered spot, but more often you'll simply be invited to choose any place you like.

Conveniences to Expect in a Camp

The universal characteristic of New Zealand motor camps is cleanliness. Whether the camp is simple or deluxe, everything will be freshly painted and scrubbed and scrupulously immaculate, without a shred of litter or speck of dirt anywhere. Every campground will, of course, have one or more buildings with toilets and hot showers. Your Kiwi neighbor will refer to these as "the ablutions" or "the amenities." There will also be a community kitchen with refrigerator, stove, and sometimes even a microwave. There will be a laundry room, a television lounge, often a little grocery store, and a playground with a trampoline. On the volcanic plateau there will usually be hot mineral springs or a jacuzzi (a "spa pool") for a soothing soak before bed. If the camp is on a bay or a lake, there may be boats for hire. Your host will be eager to direct you to the local wonders and to help with bookings and telephone calls. (Those little cabins and extra trailers you see around the camp are overnight accommodations for car travelers who want an inexpensive alternative to motels. You'll see a few tent campers, too, usually with bicycles.)

Motorcamp Etiquette

People are friendly in motor camps, but also careful not to intrude on one another's privacy. Chatting with other campers is a delightful way to find out about road conditions and worthwhile sights on tomorrow's journey. You will, of course, keep your radio and voices low (we Americans tend to talk more loudly than other nationalities, we notice) and you'll take care not to leave litter, just as you would at home. But be warned that Kiwis are especially offended by campers who let their waste water spill out on the campsite. Since few motorhomes here are equipped with holding tanks, you must be sure to put the bucket supplied with your vehicle under your outlet pipe as soon as you arrive and dump it in the proper drain in the morning. If you want to go off sightseeing or to town for the evening, leave your bucket (empty) to reserve your spot,

Laundry

All motor camps have laundry rooms with big new Maytag washers, but dryers of strange unknown brands. This makes for a peculiarly frustrating washday, The washer whizzes your clothes clean for NZ$1.50 in half an hour, and then the dryer takes three or four thirty-minute cycles at fifty cents a pop to finish the load, while you fidget impatiently to be off. Still, it beats searching for the very scarce laundromats or resorting to the universal European campwash method of stringing a line between two trees after a session at the community washtub. We also appreciate the convenience of campground irons and ironing boards (or would, if all our clothes weren't permanent press).

Water

The water supply everywhere in New Zealand is perfectly safe. Your campsite will have a spigot and a hose nearby and you can fill your motorhome kitchen water tank from it with impunity. Varying with the size of your rig and the amount of dishwashing you do in it, you'll probably need a fill-up every second or third day. Some camps also have designated car wash areas where you can hose off the dust of hard travel.

Other Patterns

Motor camps that are part of the "Top Ten Holiday Park" network offer a discount of 10 percent if you present a voucher from a previous stay with one of their member camps. They then give you another voucher good for 10 percent on your next Top Ten—and so on.

Nearly all motor camps in New Zealand are run by private owners or by cities and fit the pattern described above. However, occasionally you may come across wilderness camping places managed by the national government which come closer to the American model. These are situated in remote scenic areas and have only picnic tables, water, and chemical toilets. There are no attendants. After a night's stay you deposit the small posted fee in an "honesty box."

Freecamping

In Europe and the United States, where campgrounds are sometimes far apart ard quality is uneven, we often just stop by the side of the road to freecamp (or "boondock" as some American RVers call it). In New Zealand we find this a less tempting alternative—partly because the motor camps are so good and partly because the highway rest areas do not have toilets. However, once in a while you may want to try freecamping if the camps are all full at high season, if you've been caught at dusk far from a town if you want to economize, or if you just want to experience the nocturnal solitude of seacoast or fern forest. This is perfectly safe and legal if you don't park on private property, but be careful not to pollute the ecology by your overnight presence.

Campervan Choreography

If you and your travelmate(s) have never lived together in a motorhome, it will take a couple of days of shakedown before everything goes smoothly, especially if your rig is small. Neatness and organization are essential, even if that's not your natural style. Agree on a place for each category (clothes, shoes, laundry, toiletries, dishes, food, books and maps, sports equipment) and always put things away as soon as you're through with them. Try to stow everything so that there is nothing you repeatedly have to climb over and shift around. This is a good reason to bring only soft, foldable suitcases. Move slowly and predictably when you're cooking to avoid the danger of hot spills at close quarters. Divide up the routine morning tasks so that you can get on the road quickly without discussion. And try to be extra sensitive to your partner's needs and moods.

A technique that works for us is borrowed from the Japanese knack for creating psychological distance in crowded circumstances. When one of us needs a moment of privacy, we say, "Please go in the other room." Then the partner is obligated to turn around, stare out the window or at the wall, and mentally absent himself or herself for the necessary amount of time, until called back. It sounds silly, but this small piece of courtesy is one of the reasons we're able to live together happily in a small van for months at a time.

Motor Camp Evenings

So there you are, snugly ensconced in camp, dinner eaten and the dishes washed up, and three hours until bedtime. What to do with no television to while away that time? True, you might go to the camp telly lounge and stare at one of the two rather dull New Zealand channels. But better to invite the nice couple in the next camper over for coffee and conversation. Or go for a moonlight stroll around the town—perhaps drop in at the pub to meet the locals. You also might write postcards or keep a nightly journal of your travel impressions. Or rediscover listening to the radio. New Zealand has several excellent stations, such as National Radio and Radio New Zealand, that broadcast not only a wide range of music but also engrossing plays and discussions. (Their frequencies change from town to town, but they're worth seeking out on the dial.)

And you can always read. The *New Zealand Herald* is probably the best newspaper, and is wonderfully revealing of the quality of life here. As for books, we find that reading out loud is a fine pleasure that has undeservedly been forgotten. On the road we try to pick a book that will give added richness to our perception of the country that we are visiting. Once Huck Finn accompanied us all the way down the Mississippi and another time our dreams in Greece were full of bronze-clad warriors from our reading of *The Iliad*. In New Zealand you might sample the works of Janet Frame, Maurice Gee, or Witi Ihimaera.

MOTOR CAMP DIRECTORY
North Island

NORTHLAND

Dargaville

> Baylys Beach Motor Camp
> Seaview Road, off S.H. 12
> Phone (0884) 6349

> Selwyn Park Motor Camp
> Onslow Street
> Phone (0884) 8296

Kaitaia

> Dyers Motel & Auto Park
> 69 South Road
> Phone 39

> Ninety Mile Beach Holiday Park
> 18 km north of Kaitala In Waipapakauri
> Phone (0889) 77 298

Kerikeri

> Aranga Holiday Park
> Kerikeri Road, 500 m south of town center
> Phone (0887) 79 326

Mangawhai

> Mangawhai River Holiday Park
> Black Swamp Road
> Phone (0846) 68 825
>
> Mangawhai Village Motor Camp
> Kaiwaka-Mangawhai Road
> Phone (0846) 68 542

Mangonui, Doubtless Bay

> Coopers Beach Holiday Park
> 2 km north of Mangonui on S.H. 10
> Phone 60 597 Mangonui
>
> Hihi Beach Motor Park
> 5 km down Hihi Road, off S.H. 10, 7 km south of Mangonui
> Phone 60 307 Mangonui

Paihip, Bay of Islands

> Falls Motor Inn & Caravan Park
> Puketona Road, Haruru Falls
> Phone (0885) 27 816
>
> Lily Pond Holiday Park
> Puketona Road, 6 km north of Paihia, past Haruru Falls
> Phone (0885) 27 646
>
> Smiths Holiday Camp
> Paihia-Opua Road
> Phone (0885) 27 678
>
> Twin Pines Motor Camp
> Haruru Falls
> Phone (0885) 27 322

Russell, Bay of Islands

> Orongo Bay Motor Camp
> Between Russell and car ferry from Opua
> Phone (0885) 37 704

Russell Holiday Park
Long Beach Road
Phone (0885) 37 826

Tauranga Bay (north)

Tauranga Bay Motor Camp
18 km north of Kaeo on Whangaroa Bay
Phone 59 Kaeo

Wellsford

Pakiri Surf Beach Motor Camp & Motel
Phone (0846) 26 199

Whangarei

Alpha Caravan Park & Mini Motel
34 Tarewa Road
Phone (089) 489 867

Blue Heron Holiday Park
Scott Road off Whangarei Heads Road
Phone (089) 62 293

Harbour Lights Holiday Resort
128 One Tree Point Road, Marsden Point turn off
Phone (089) 27 651

The Nook Beach Resort
25 km east of Whangarei, off Whangarei Heads Highway
Phone (08921) 746

Otaika Motel & Caravan Park
136 Otaika Road, on S.H. 1 south side of Whangarei City
opposite Otaika shopping centre
Phone (089) 481 459

Tropicana Holiday Park & Motels
Whangarei Heads Road
Phone (089) 60 687

Whangarei Falls Auto Park

Kiripaka Road, Tikipunga
Phone (089) 70 609

Whangaruru

Oakura Motels & Caravan Park
50 km northeast of Whangarei on the coast road to Russell
Phone (08936) 803

AUCKLAND AREA

Auckland

Avondale Motor Park
46 Bollard Avenue, off New North Road between Mt. Albert and Avondale
Phone (09) 887 228

Manukau Central Caravan Park
902 Great South Road, 1½ km south of Manukau City turnoff
Phone (09) 266 8016

Meadowcourt Motel
630 Great South Road, Manukau City
Phone (09) 278 5612

North Shore Caravan Park
52 Northcote Road, Whangarei Lane over Harbour Bridge, 4 km north, left into Northcote Road (not Northcote-Birkenhead), Takapuna
Phone (09) 419 1320

Remuera Motor Lodge & Camping Ground
16 Minto Road, Green Lane turnoff from S.H. 1
Phone (09) 545 126

Takapuna Tourist Court
22 The Promenade, on Takapuna Beach
Phone (09) 497 909

Clarks Beach

Clarks Beach Holiday Park
Torker Road Extension, 25 km from Papakura
Phone 685 Waiau Pa

Clevedon

Orere Point Motor Camp
On Firth of Thames coastline on road to Coromandel
Peninsula
Phone (09) 292 2774

Henderson

Tui Glen Holiday Tourist Park
Edmonton Road
Phone (09) 836 8978

Parakai

Aquatic Park Holiday Camp
Parkhurst Road and Springs Road
Phone (0880) 8998
Mineral Park Motel
Parakai Avenue
Phone (0880) 8856

Port Waikato

Port Waikato Motor Camp
Mansuell Road, 26 km off S.H. 22
Phone (085) 298 57

Ramarama

South Auckland Caravan Park
Great South Road, 32 km south of Auckland
Phone (09) 294 8121

Waiuku

Waiuku Sandspit Motor Camp
Sandspit Road, 65 km southwest of Auckland
Phone (085) 59 913

COROMANDEL/WAIKATO

Cambridge

Cambridge Domain Motor Camp
Scott Street, Leamington
Phone (07 127) 5649

Hamilton

Hamilton East Tourist Court
61 Cameron Road
Phone (071) 66 220

Kawhia

Kawhia Camping Ground
Moke Street, on Karewa Beach
Phone (08225) 727

Ngaruawahia

Waingaro Hot Springs
Waingaro Road
Phone (071) 254 761

Otorohanga

Otorohanga Motor Camp
Domain Drive next to the Kiwi House and public swimming pool
Phone (08133) 8214

Pauanui

The Glade Holiday Resort
Pauanui Beach, Tairua Harbour
Phone (0843) 87 308

Te Puru

Boomerang Motor Camp
Thames Coast, 11 km north of Thames
Phone (0843) 78 879

Thames

Dickson Park Motor Camp
Victoria Street
Phone (0843) 87 308

Waiomu

Waiomu Bay Holiday Park
Thames Coast, 13 km north of Thames

Whangamata

Pinefield Holiday Park
Fort Road
Phone (0816) 58 791

Whitianga

Buffalo Beach Tourist Park
Eyre Street
Phone (0843) 65 854

Cooks Beach Motor Camp
Cooks Beach
Phone (0843) 65 469

Hahei Holidays Tourist Park
Hahei Beach
Phone (084363) 889

Mercury Bay Motor Camp
125 Albert St.
Phone (0843) 65 579

Whitianga Holiday Park
North end of Buffalo Beach
Phone (0843) 65 896

BAY OF PLENTY

Kati Kati

Sapphire Springs
Hot Springs Road, 3 km south of Kati Kati on S.H. 2
Phone (075) 490 768

Matata

Murphy's Motor Camp
S.H. 2, 2 km west of Matata
Phone (076) 22 136

Mount Maunganui

Cosy Corner Motor Camp
40 Ocean Beach Road
Phone (075) 55 899

Golden Grove Motor Park
73 Girven Road, off Mt. Maunganui Highway
Phone (075) 55 821

Omanu Beach Holiday Park
70 Ocean Beach Road
Phone (075) 55 968

Ohope

"Englands" Ohope Beach Holiday Park
Harbour Road
Phone (076) 24 460

Surf 'n' Sand Holiday Park
211 Pohutukawa Ave.
Phone (076) 24 884

Omokoroa Beach

Omokoroa Tourist Park
Beach Road
Phone 480 857

Opotiki

Island View Family Holiday
Appleton Road, Waiotahi Beach
Phone (076) 57 519

Papamoa

Papamoa Beach Holiday Park
535 Papamoa Beach Road
Phone (075) 420 816

Tauranga

> Plummers Point Caravan Park & Pools
> 19 km north of Tauranga on S.H. 2
> Phone 460 669
>
> Silver Birch Motor Park
> 101 Turrett Road, on main Tauranga-Mt. Maunganui
> Hwy. on harbour's edge

Te Araroa

> Te Araroa Holiday Park
> Mid-way Hicks Bay-Te Araroa, East Cape
> Phone (07944) 873

Te Puke

> Te Puke Holiday Park
> S.H. 2, north side of town
> Phone (075) 739 866

Waihau Bay

> Heron Creek Holiday Park
> Oruaiti Beach
> Phone (07653) 844

Waihi Beach

> Athenree Motor Camp
> Northern end of Tauranga Harbor
> Waihi Beach South
> Phone (0816) 45 600
>
> Beachaven Caravan Park
> 21 Leo Street
> Phone (0816) 45 505
>
> Bowentown Motor Camp
> Southern end Seaforth Road, Waihi Beach South
> Phone (0816) 45 381
>
> Waihi Beach Holiday Park
> 15 Main Road
> Phone (0816) 45 504

Waihi Motor Camp
6 Waitete Road
Phone (08163) 7654

Whakatane

Awakeri Hot Springs
Rotorua-Whakatane Hwy.
Phone (076) 49 117

Whakatane Family Motor Camp
McGarvey Road
Phone (076) 88 694

ROTORUA AREA

Blue Lake

Blue Lake Holiday Park
Tarawera Road, Lake Tikitapu
Phone (073) 28 120

Hannahs Bay

Moana Auto Park
Lee Road, left off S.H. 30
Phone (073) 56 240

Lake Rotoma

Merge Lodge Caravan Park
Lake Rotoma, on P.H. 30
Phone (07320) 831

Rotoma Holiday Park
Manawahe Road (or Soda Springs Road)
Phone (07320) 815

Ngongotaha

Lodge Motorcourt
School and Hall roads
Phone (073) 74 429

Ngongotaha Motel and Caravan Park

22 Beaumont Road
Phone (073) 74 289

Waiteti Trout Stream Holiday Park
14 Okona Crescent
Phone (073) 74749

Willowhaven Holiday Park
31 Beaumont Road
Phone (093) 74 092

Okere Falls

Taheke Lakeside Holiday Park
Okere Road, Lake Rotoiti
Phone (073) 24 860

Rotorua

Cosy Cottage Motor Camp
67 Whittaker Road
Phone (073) 83793

Holdens Bay Holiday Park
21 Robinson Avenue, 6 km from Central Post Office on
    P.H. 30, third turn left past Shell Te Ngae Motors
Phone (073) 55421

Lakeside Motor Camp
Whittaker Road
Phone (073) 81 693

Redwood Park Motel & Caravan Park
5 Tarawera Road
Phone (073) 55421

Rotorua Thermal Motor Camp
Old Taupo Road (South End)
Phone (073) 88 385

Thermal Lodge
60 Tarewa Road
Phone (073) 70931

Tikitere

Kiwi Ranch
Christian holiday camp opposite Hells Gate on P.H. 30
Phone (073) 56 799

EAST COAST (FROM EAST CAPE)

Gisborne

Waikanae Beach Motor Camp
Grey Street
Phone (079) 75 634

Hastings

Raceview Motel & Holiday Park
307 Gascoigne Street
Phone (070) 88 837
Windsor Park Motor Camp
Windsor Avenue
Phone (070) 86 692

Havelock North

Arataki Holiday Park
Te Mata Road, from Havelock North to Arataki Road
Phone (070) 777 479

Mahia

Blue Bay Motor Camp
Opoutama Beach
Phone (072425) 867
Mahia Beach Motels & Motor Camp
Mahia Peninsula
Phone (072425) 830

Napier

Kennedy Park Complex
Storkey Street, off Kennedy Road

Phone (070) 439 126

Taradale Holiday Park
470 Gloucester Street, 1 km south of Taradale Post Office
Phone (070) 442 732

Westshore Holiday Camp
Main Road, Westshore
Phone (070) 359 456

Te Awanga

Beachcrest Motel & Tourist Flats
4 Leyland Road
Phone (070) 750 170

Waimarama

Waimarama Holiday Park
32 km southeast of Hastings
Phone (070) 786 836

Waipawa

Two Mac's Seaside Camp
42 km east of Waipawa, turn off at Tamumu Road, Waipawa
Phone (0728) 63 524

Waipukurau

Waipukurau Motor Camp
River Terrace, S.H. 2
Phone (0728) 88 184

Wairoa

Wairoa Municipal Motor Camp
18 Marine Parade
Phone (0724) 6301

CENTRAL PLATEAU

Raetihi

Raetihi Motor Camp
S.H. 4, at junction of P.H. 49
Phone (0658) 54 176

Reporoa

Golden Springs Holiday Park
Midway between Rotorua and Taupo on S.H. 5
Phone (073) 38 280

Taihape

Abba Motor Camp
Old Abattoir Road, 3 km north of Taihape Post Office
off S.H. 1
Phone (0658) 80 718

Taupo

Acacia Holiday Park
Acacia Bay Road
Phone (9074) 85159

Auto Park
16 Rangatira Street
Phone (074) 84 272

De Bretts Family Leisure Park
1 km from Lake Taupo on the Taupo-Napier Hwy.
Phone (074) 88 559

Hilltop Motor Caravan Park
39 Puriri Street
Phone (074) 85247

Lake Taupo Holiday Park
Centennial Drive (Upper Spa Road)
Phone (074) 86 860

Taupo Motor Camp

Redoubt Street
Phone (074) 86 600

Tokaanu

Oasis Motels & Caravan Park
P.H. 41
Phone (0746) 8569

Tokoroa

Lochmaben Caravan Park
55 Lochmaben Road
Phone (080) 69 449

Tongariru National Park

Whakapapa Motor Camp
Across from Visitors Center

Turangi

Motutere Bay Caravan Park
34 km from Taupo on S.H. 1
Phone (0746) 8963

Tauranga-Taupo Lodge
11 km north of Turangi on southeastern side of Lake
    Taupo
Phone (074) 8385 or 8386

Tongariro Outdoor Centre
Ohuanga Road
Phone (0746) 7492

Turangi Holiday Park
Ohuanga Road
Phone (0746) 8754

TARANAKI/WANGANUI

Hawera

King Edward Park
Waihi Road
Phone (062) 86414

New Plymouth

Aaron Court Motel & Caravan Park
S.H. 3, south side
Phone (067) 88 712

Belt Road Motor Camp
2 Belt Road, 1.5 km west of City Centre
Phone (067) 80 228

Fitzroy Beach Motor Camp
Beach Street
Phone (067) 82 870

Princes Tourist Court
29 Princes Street, Fitzroy
Phone (067) 82 566

Stratford

Stratford Campsite
King Edward Park, 10 Page Street
Phone (0663) 6440

Waitara

Marine Park Motor Camp
Centennial Avenue
Phone (0674) 7121

Wanganui

Aramoho Park Motor Camp
460 Somme Parade, city side bank of Wanganui River
Phone (064) 38 402

Avro Motel & Caravan Court
36 Alma Road, off New Plymouth bypass
Phone (064) 55 279

Castlecliff Motor Camp
Rangiora Street, Castlecliff Beach
Phone (064) 42 227

WELLINGTON AREA

Bulls

Bridge Motor Lodge
2 Bridge Street, ½ km south of Bulls on S.H. 1
Phone (0652) 48 894

Castlepoint

Castlepoint Motor Camp
65 km northeast of Masterton
Phone (05926) 660

Levin

Playford Park Motor Camp
38 Parker Avenue
Phone (069) 83 549

Manakau

Tatum Park
S.H. 1, 10 km south of Levin
Phone (06926) 799

Masterton

Mawley Park
Oxford Street, adjacent to river near Queen Elizabeth
Park
Phone (059) 86 454

Otaki Beach

Capitol Holiday Park
Tasman Road, 4 km off S.H. 1
Phone (069) 48 121

Paekakariki

Batchelors Holiday Park
Cross railway tracks, right at post office, 1.5 km on Wellington Road to Park
Phone (058) 28 292

Palmerston North

Palmerston North Municipal Motor Camp
133 Dittmer Drive off Ruha Street
Phone (063) 80 349

Paraparaumu

Lindale Motor Home & Caravan Park
S.H. 1, 45 min. north of Wellington
Phone (058) 88 046

Waikanae

Waikanae Bush Camp
Reikorangi, Waikanae-Upper Hutt Road 2 km from Waikanae
Phone (058) 35 31

Hydrabad Holiday Park
Forest Road, east of S.H. 1, north of Levin
Phone (069) 84 941

Wellington

Hutt Park Holiday Village
95 Hutt Park Road, Moera, Lower Hutt (see Itinerary chapter for map and detailed directions)
Phone 685 913

South Island

NELSON/MARLBOROUGH

Blenheim

Al Holiday Park
78 Grove Road, S.H. 1
Phone (057) 83667

Blenheim Motor Camp
27 Budge Street
Phone (057) 87 419

Duncannon Caravan Park
St. Andrews, 2 km south of Blenheim on Main South
Hwy.
Phone (057) 88 193
Spring Creek Holiday Park
Rapaura Road, Spring Creek, 6 km north of Blenheim,
Turn inland at Spring Creek Hotel.
Phone (05725) 893

Mapua

Mapua Leisure Park
Toru Street
Phone (05422) 666

Marlborough Sounds

Momorangi Bay Motor Camp
Queen Charlotte Drive
Queen Charlotte Sound

Murchison

Riverview Motor Camp
2 km north of Murchison
Phone 115M

Nelson

Maitai Motor Camp
Adjacent to Municipal Golf Course

Richmond Holiday Park
29 Gladstone Road, Richmond
Phone (0544) 7323

Tahuna Beach Holiday Park
70 Beach Road, Tahuna
Phone (054) 85 159

Waimea Town & Country Club Caravan Park
345 Queen Street, Richmond
Phone (0544) 6476

Picton

    Alexanders Motor Park
    Canterbury Street, 3 min. drive from ferry
    Phone (057) 36 378
    Blue Anchor Holiday Park
    64 Waikawa Road
    Phone (057) 37 212
    Parklands Marina Holiday Village
    Beach Road, Waikawa Bay
    Phone (057) 343

WEST COAST

Fox Glacier

    Fox Glacier Motor Park
    Lake Matheson Road
    Phone 821

Franz Josef

    Franz Josef Motor Camp
    Main road
    Phone 766

Greymouth

    Greymouth Seaside Holiday Park
    Chesterfield, signs ½ km past Greymouth Hospital on
        Main South Road
    Phone (027) 6618
    South Beach Motor Park
    318 Main South Road, 6 km south of post office
    Phone (02726) 768

Haast

    Haast Motor Camp
    14.5 km south on Jackson Bay Road
    Phone 860 Haast

Hokitika

> Hokitika Holiday Park
> Livingstone Street, on Borough East boundary adjacent
>   to Main South Hwy.

Westport

> Westport Howard Park Holiday Camp
> Domett Street, signposted from post office
> Phone (0289) 7043

CANTERBURY

Amberley

> Delhaven Motels & Caravan Park
> 124 Main Road
> Phone (0504) 48 550

Ashburton

> Coronation Park
> 778 East Street
> Phone (053) 6603

Banks Peninsula

> Akaroa Holiday Park
> Morgan Road, Akaroa off S.H. 75
> Phone 471 AK
>
> Le Bons Bay Motor Camp
> Valley Road, Le Bons Bay
> Phone 8533 Akaroa
>
> Purau Bay Motor Camp
> Diamond Harbour
> Phone (03) 294 702

Christchurch

> Amber Park Mini Motel & Caravan Park
> 308 Blenheim Road, 4 km south of city center
> Phone (03) 483 327

Meadow Park
39 Meadow Street, on S.H. 1, 4 km north of city center
Phone (03) 529 176

Russley Park Motor Camp
372 Yaldhurst Road, on P.H. 73, 4 km from airport
Phone (03) 427 021

South New Brighton Motor Camp
Halsey Street (off Estuary Road), South Brighton
Phone (03) 889 844

Hanmer Springs

Mountain View Holiday Park
Main Road
Phone (0515) 7113

Kaiapoi

Blue Skies
12 Williams Street, 1 km south of S.H. 1, south end of
    town
Phone (03) 278 398

Pineacres Motor Camp
Main North Road
Phone (0327) 7421

Kaikoura

Kaikoura Motels & Caravan Park
11-15 Beach Road, on main hwy.
Phone (0513) 5999

Methven

Methven A & P Caravan Park
Barkers Road, in the Methven Showgrounds
Phone (053) 28 005

Prebbleton

Prebbleton Holiday Park
18 Blakes Road, 12 km southwest from Christchurch
    center
Phone (03) 497 861

Rakaia

Rakaia River Holiday Park
Main South Road
Phone (053) 27 257

Spencerville

Spencer Park
14 km northeast of Christchurch
Phone (03298) 721

SOUTH CANTERBURY/OTAGO

Dunedin

Aaron Lodge Motel & Caravan Park
162 Kaikorai Valley Road, 4 min. to city center
Phone (024) 64 725

Larnach Castle Lodge
Larnach Castle, 20 min. from Dunedin
Phone (024) 761 302

Leith Valley Touring Park
103 Malvern Street, adjacent to Northern Motorway
Phone (024) 74 936

Tahuna Park Seaside Camp
41 Victoria Road, adjacent to beach in A & P
Showgrounds
Phone (024) 54 690

Waitati Farmlands Camper/Caravan Park
Waitati Valley Road, 15 min. north of Dunedin
Phone (024) 22 730

Fairlie

C.J. Talbot Motor Camp
On P.H. 79
Phone 8475 Fairlie

Geraldine

Geraldine Motor Camp
Corner P.H. 79 and Hislop Street
Phone (056) 38 860

Glenavy

Glentaki Holiday Camp
S.H. 1 north of Waitaki Bridge
Phone (0519) 888

Lake Tekapo

Lake Tekapo Motor Camp
Phone (05056) 825

Lawrence

Gold Park Motor Camp
Harrington Street
Phone Lawrence 185

Mount Cook

Glentanner Park
P.H. 80, 20 km from Mt. Cook Village
Phone 855 Mt. Cook

Omarama

Glenburn Park
P. H. 83, 7 km east of town
Phone (02984) 411

Omarama Caravan Park
Junction Hwys. 8 and 83
Phone (02984) 875

Otematata

Otematata Lodge & Camping Ground
East Road
Phone (02982) 826

Ranfurly

> Ranfurly Camping Ground
> 8 Reade Street
> Phone 70

Timaru

> Selwyn Holiday Park
> 144 Selwyn Street. Turn into Hobb Street, off Evan
> Street to entrance.
> Phone (056) 47 690

Twizel

> Ruataniwha Motor Camp
> 4 km south of town on the shore of Lake Ruataniwha
> Phone (05620) 613

Waihola

> Lake Waihola Holiday Park
> 100 m off S.H. 1
> Phone (02997) 8908

CENTRAL OTAGO/SOUTHLAND

Alexandra

> Alexandra Holiday Camp
> Manuherikia Road
> Phone (0294) 88 297
> Pine Lodge Holiday Camp
> Ngapara Street
> Phone (0294) 88 861

Arrowtown

> Arrowtown Caravan Park
> 47 Devon Street
> Phone (029420) 838

Cromwell

Sunhaven Motor Camp
Alpha Street
Phone 50 164

Glenorchy

Genorchy Holiday Park
2 Oban Street, at head of Lake Wakatipu
Phone (0294) 29 939

Invercargill

Invercargill Caravan Park
20 Victoria Avenue
Phone (021) 88787

Kingston

Kingston Caravan Park
Terminal of vintage steam train *Kingston Flyer*
Phone (02283) 541 GTN

Lumsden

Mossburn Country Park
Five Rivers Road
Phone (0228) 6030

Manapouri

Manapouri Lakeview Motels & Motor Park
20 km south of Te Anau on Manapouri-Te Anau Hwy.
Phone (02296) 624

Milford

Milford Lodge
Milford Road, 1 km before town

Murray Gunn's Motor Camp
Milford Road, Lower Hollyford Road.

Queenstown

Creeksyde Camper Van Park
Robins Road

Phone (0294) 29 447

Frankton Motor Camp
Phone (0294) 27 252

Queenstown Holiday Park
Arthurs Point
Phone (0294) 29 306

Queenstown Motor Park
Phone (0294) 27 252

Roxburgh

Roxburgh Motor Camp
11 Teviot Street
Phone (0294) 48 093

Te Anau

Te Anau Motor Park
Te Anau-Manapouri Road
Phone (0229) 7457

Te Anau Mountain View Caravan & Cabin Park
Mokonui Street & Te Anau Terrace
Phone (0229) 7462

Wanaka

Lake Hawea Motor Camp
Lake Hawea, 10 min. from town
Phone (02943) 8767

Penrith Park
Beacon Pt. Road
Phone (02942) 7009

Wanaka Motor Park
212 Brownston Street
Phone (02943) 7883

Wanaka Pleasant Lodge Tourist Park
Glendue Bay Road
Phone (02943) 7360

CHAPTER 5

Eating in the Best Places

New Zealand has superb food, but you'll never know it if you take all your meals in small cafes and tea shops. Unfortunately the British heritage has left its mark on the average Kiwi's attitudes in the kitchen. The philosophy of home cooking can be summed up in the menu formula "meat and two veg," and modest eateries serve greasy chips with deep-fat-fried everything or make peculiarly misguided attempts at European cliches like quiche. If you persist in playing restaurant roulette on the road you're going to be in for some unpleasant surprises.

However, a number of fine eating places In cities and tourist resorts serve food that does justice to New Zealand's bounty. European-trained Kiwi chefs have recently made progress in developing a national cuisine based on sophisticated use of the country's wealth of seafood, gloriously fresh vegetables and exotic fruits, superb dairy products, and, of course, the world-famous lamb. To dine in these establishments can be a uniquely pleasurable—if somewhat expensive—travel adventure.

But you will often be in small towns or remote scenic areas when dinnertime comes around—since the beauty of the countryside is what you came to see—and nowhere near a good restaurant. For this reason, and because a steady diet of rich gourmet food is unhealthy for both your body and your wallet, we suggest that you make good use of that cute little kitchen in your motorhome. Food shopping and cooking are interesting on the road. The following pages will get you started on exploring the culinary possibilities of seafood and vegetables and fruits that grow nowhere else in the world.

First, however, a bit more about eating out before we launch into a discussion of eating in.

Restaurant Etiquette

You'll need to get dressed up for that restaurant dinner (another reason why you probably won't want to do it every night). Many first-class establishments require that gentlemen wear coat and tie and ladies wear dresses. Kiwis make a whole evening's entertainment out of a night at a fine restaurant, usually arriving about seven, eating and drinking in a leisurely manner, and staying on and on over cordials and conversation until the place closes. So don't be annoyed to see parties of diners lingering over coffee while you wait for a table, and don't fault the waitress if the service seems slow. Relax and get into the Kiwi rhythm of the thing.

Some Other Customs

There are two kinds of restaurants in the eyes of the law: licensed and BYO. The first is allowed to serve liquor, and the second, as the initials spell out, is "Bring Your Own." You arrive with wine bottle in hand, and the waiter chills it if necessary and pours it with the meal. There is usually a small corkage fee, no more than one or two dollars.

There is no tipping. That's right—no tipping. Unless, of course, you've asked the waiter to do some really exceptional service, and even then he or she will be embarrassed if you offer more than $2NZ, regardless of the size of your tab. A typically egalitarian Kiwi custom, if you've developed an especially pleasant rapport with your waiter, is to invite him to join your table later on in the evening.

A few words of vocabulary clarification might be in order. Courses progress through starters, entrees, and mains. (Notice that the entree is not the central event.) Familar vegetables may be listed by unfamiliar names, such as marrow (squash), courgette (zucchini), or capsicums (bell peppers). And if the waiter has been neglectful in the table setting, ask for a "serviette" rather than a napkin unless you really do want to be brought a diaper.

Specialties

Some delectable New Zealand dishes can only be sampled in restaurants, either because they are beyond the reach of a camper kitchen or because the ingredients are not available in food stores. Venison, for instance, appears in butcher shops but rarely and then only as sausage, but is featured on many restaurant menus, Wild boar is equally limited. Whitebait—delectable little new-hatched smelt—is on the market only in the spring but some restaurants seem to have a secret year-round supply. Rack of lamb, of course, you can't attempt without an oven, but what would a visit to sheep country be without at least once enjoying this queenly feast. Pumpkin soup, an autumn specialty, is impossible without a blender, so you'll want to try it in a cafe. The shellfish *toheroa,* reportedly the epitome of New Zealand gastronomy, can be dug at certain beaches for only a brief season. Even if you did manage to be in the right place at the right time, preparing the nasty black thing inside the shell is extremely intimidating (it was the instruction to "Press out the two teeth" that did me in). But served up nicely in a pretty soup, it and its cousin the *tuatua* are a good reason for eating out.

Prices

The bad news is that the bill in a fine New Zealand restaurant can be at least twice what you'd expect to pay at home, and tallies of NZ$100 per couple are not unusual. But remember that tax (or G.S.T.) is included in the price listed on the menu, and there is no tip or parking charge. Your Kiwi friends will explain these high prices quite reasonably by pointing out that a small isolated population does not generate the numbers for quantity marketing, and "everyone is paid a living wage." To know what you're getting into ahead of time, equip yourself with a copy of *Michael Guy's Eating Out,* an amusingly candid listing of restaurants in Kiwi-land, both good and bad.

Takeaways and Other Fast Food

A ubiquitous New Zealand institution, the takeaway shop is fun for an occasional lunch or snack, The basic assumption is that you'll take the food away someplace else to eat it (although occasionally there are picnic tables outside in the sun). If you ask for your food "to go" or "to take out" or "to carry out" you'll get nothing but a blank look. The standard takeaway fare is fish and chips—deep-fat batter-fried snapper and french fries—done up hot to order and wrapped in newspaper for greaseless carrying. The fish is always good, but the oil is sometimes not as fresh as it should be, Other deep-fried takeaway items are mussels and scallops in season, artificial crab sticks, and curry roll (like a long Chinese egg roll). "Hot pies" are often sold both at takeaway shops and anyplace else with a counter big enough for a microwave. These are meat pies, usually hamburger (called "mince") even though labeled "steak and onion" or "steak and kidney." They can be pretty good if they're homemade, and make a comforting lunch with a cup of tea on a nippy day.

Cooked chicken, or "chooks," is sometimes offered for takeaway, but can be very expensive by U.S. standards. And yes, American franchises have begun to infiltrate in the shape of Colonel Sanders, Pizza Hut, and of course, McDonald's.

Food Events

A hangi, or Maori luau is an experience not to be missed. Shellfish, meats, and vegetables are steamed in an underground oven, and traditional Maori songs and dances are performed after the feast. The place to do this is in Rotorua, at any of the major hotels.

"Devonshire tea" is another food event where ambience is as important as the menu. Best eaten on a grey afternoon, this evocative meal should feature tiny sandwiches and fresh-baked scones with whipped cream and raspberry jam. It should be served with ceremony on flowery china in a walnut-paneled room with lace curtains on high windows. Turkey Red, a charming tearoom in a 121-year-old mansion, does it exactly right. (Highway 2 north of Greytown.) The Stone Cottage in Arrowtown is also famous for its Devonshire teas.

On a farm stay you'll probably be served a bountiful dinner of roast lamb with home-grown vegetables, topped off with the famous Kiwi meringue dessert called pavlova* *(see the recipes at the end of this chapter for directions for this and other starred dishes)*.

Wine-growing regions like Hawke's Bay sponsor "wine trails" for sampling their product. Orchards, too, sometimes have tours (you can't miss the Giant Kiwi Slice near Te Puke). Agricultural and Pastoral Shows (or A & P Shows) have cooking competitions and food displays along with all the other goings-on associated with a state fair. And many food-producing regions have annual festivals to glorify their main crop. Ask the NZTP for the booklet *Taste New Zealand* for a complete list of all these events.

**Your Motorhome Kitchen
—the Very Best Eating Place**

Meanwhile, let's see what you've got to work with in your own kitchen on wheels. The built-in range, unlike those smelly Coleman stoves that need endless pumping, lights at the turn of a knob with clean, quiet bottled propane. It will probably have one burner and a little broiler (known in Kiwi as a "griller"). There will be running water, a stainless steel sink and drain, and a refrigerator that runs on both car battery and electricity. Unless you've chosen the deluxe model you won't have hot water, but it takes only a minute to boil up a potful for dishwashing. Your rental company will have provided you with ample dishes and cooking equipment, but you may want to tuck a favorite dish or tool from home into your luggage. I, for instance, can't cook a note without my pet knife and black iron skillet, and David is unhappy drinking coffee from anything but his special mug.

The motorhome company will have supplied you with salt and pepper, tea, and instant coffee, and sugar. On your first shopping trip you'll probably also want to pick up other staples: bread, milk, butter, oil, a roll of paper towels, maybe some cheese and eggs. Of course you don't want to lay in a complete spice shelf, but we find mustard, soy sauce, and curry powder very useful condiments in relation to New Zealand foods. (The latter is best bought in Auckland, where there is a sizeable Indian population to insist on the real thing.) Notice that prices for meat, fish, and produce are by the kilogram (kg) which is about two pounds, so at first glance they will seem rather high.

Now you're all set to produce a quick and nutritious cozy supper by grilling a little steak or a nice piece of fish, steaming a vegetable or slicing a simple salad. Not to speak of breakfast coffee or tea made the way *you* like it, and spur-of-the-moment picnics. As you begin to get the hang of the thing, you'll want to play around, to try some of the new fruits and vegetables you'll see at roadside stalls and to feast on familiar foods, like lamb chops, oysters, or orange roughy, that are expensive luxuries at home but gloriously affordable here—if you cook them yourself.

Food Shopping as Adventure

As you might expect, there are supermarkets in New Zealand. They look and smell and sound just like those at home (even though they call the cart a "trolley"). Every little town has its Four Square or IGA. In cities look for larger versions of these, or the Woolworth's Super Store (no relation to the dime store of your childhood). The most relaxed shopping strategy is to use the supermarket only every three or four days to stock up on staples and hard-to-find items, and then to play it by ear on the road, letting your dinner come to you by serendipity as part of the travel adventure. When you pass through a nice town, stop off for a minute at the "butchery" or the "fishery" and pick up what looks good. Later as you drive through some lovely orchards pull over at a roadside stall, stretch your legs, have a chat with the farmer, and buy some of his just-picked vegetables and fruits. When you see a sign that says "Hot Bread" put on the brakes and succumb to fresh-baked scones or cream buns. Then when early evening comes and you settle into your grassy, shady motor camp, you're all set to lean back with a glass of wine and later assemble something tasty, rather than rushing to town to beat the 5:30 closing.

Supermarkets and other food stores generally are shut on Sunday and holidays. If you forget to plan ahead, there are alternatives. "Dairies" can be found everywhere and will be open when everything else isn't. They sell milk, butter, ice cream, plain cheese, a few groceries, and soft drinks. The campground store, too, can help out in after-hours emergencies, but their stock is limited. New Zealand has a number of summer holidays that can result in three- or even four-day weekends and tight shopping if you don't see them coming. (See Chapter 7 for a list of dates.)

Meat

On your first shopping trip you will make a wonderful discovery: *lamb chops are incredibly cheap!* You can, in all good conscience, afford to trim them down to just the delectable tender meat, cutting off most of the fat as health experts decree, leaving only enough to make a crisp brown edge around the pink-in-the-center morsel. (Now you know why we told you to be sure your motorhome had a grill.) So have two, have four—heck, have a whole dozen!

When your vision clears, you'll notice that some lamb chops are labeled "hogget." This more mature meat has a fuller flavor, ("Wethers," which you will see only rarely, is mutton.) Other cuts that are appropriate for grilling are lamb steaks and noisettes. Occasionally you'll find lamb cut for stir-fry, which makes an excellent basis for Quick Lamb Curry*.

Bacon comes in two styles, "shoulder" and "middle." Both are quite lean and make a good starting point for vegetable creations like Silverbeet with Bacon*, as well as good old BLTs. Kiwi beef is almost as tasty as American and a bit cheaper. A "Porterhouse" (which is more like a New York cut) is just the right size for motorhome cooking. Another handy cut is the so-called "wienerschnitzel," which comes both crumbed and uncrumbed. The naked version slices up nicely for a delicious Chinese Beef and Asparagus*.

Seafood

A stunning array of absolutely fresh seafood is to be found in little "fishery" shops everywhere. Varieties include the delicious John Dory and orange roughy, and more unfamiliar fish like gurnard, hapuku, trevalli, hoki, hapuka, silver snapper, and opakapaka. Try several kinds, either grilled with a little lemon and butter sauce, poached gently in wine, or sauteed Japanese-style with minced garlic and green ginger*. In early spring you'll be able to buy tiny whitebait, which tastes like crab when fried up in fritters*. The green mussels are huge, either shelled or alive in tanks. And Bluff oysters come into season in April. Scallops are wonderful from July through February and go well sauteed lightly with mushrooms in a wine and mustard sauce*. A treat to be sought out is the succulent crayfish, a kind of rock lobster. Look for the "Cooked cray" signs along Highway 1 north of Christchurch.

Fruits and Vegetables

The rich volcanic soil produces marvellously flavorful fruits and vegetables. Because it's all farm-fresh, selection is seasonal. However, there's plenty to choose from. Apples in hundreds of varieties are crisp and tangy in the fall. (We especially like Gala and Harold Red.) Superb asparagus graces the spring months, and sweet corn is cause for rejoicing in the summer. Peaches or strawberries with rich New Zealand cream are memorable. Cabbages and cauliflower are gigantic, and bell peppers grow not only red and green, but also yellow and black. (A combination of colors plus fresh pineapple makes up a spicy Capsicum Curry* to accompany those lamb chops.) The place to buy, as we have said, is at the roadside, where you'll see signs for not only "Fruits and Veges," but surprises like "Duck eggs," "Currants," or "Pick-your-own mushrooms."

New experiences are to be had in sampling the many exotic fruits. Don't be shy about asking, "How do you eat this?" (although the standard Kiwi reply is "Over ice cream"). Kiwifruit you will of course expect to find, but try also pepino (a delicate oval orange melon with a shiny yellow and purple skin), passionfruit (a hard black ball with a crispy pulp inside), horned melon or kiwona (spiky yellow outside, tangy green jelly around seeds inside), feijoa (large pineapple guava), gooseberres (paper hulls around small green-yellow globes), and nashi (crisp, juicy yellow apple-pears). If you're making a fruit salad, the Kiwi way is to top it with passionfruit pulp or bits of crystallized ginger.

Vegetables, too, can be surprising. Kumara, a kind of sweet potato, is delicious roasted with lamb or pork, or steamed in its jacket in chunks and smashed with butter and salt. New Zealand pumpkin can be orange, gray, or dark green, and looks like a squashed round pillow. The traditional cooking method is to boil it in serving pieces with the potatoes. New Zealand yams are small, like somebody's wrinkled big toe, and other such vegetables are swedes (rutabagas), buttercup squash, and taro. Silverbeet looks like gigantic Swiss chard, and is tasty and healthful shredded and cooked like spinach. The tree tomato, or tamarillo, is a shiny red egg-shaped vegetable that can be made into a tangy sauce for lamb or pork* or mixed with whipped cream* for a refreshing dessert.

Dairy Products

One glance at the deep green grass under the cows' feet will tell you why dairy products are so excellent in New Zealand. The rich milk goes into great slabs of excellent butter, natural fruit yogurts, and fine honest cheeses. The white cheddar is most common in shops, and it is excellent in open-face tomato-cheese sandwiches* or melted into pasta (see Comfort Noodles*). Look also for "dairy custard" in cartons, a milk-and-egg dessert that goes very well over fruit or plain cake.

Baked Goods

Plastic-wrapped bread is even worse in New Zealand than it is at home. Luckily there are lots of bakeries with "hot bread" signs. The "wholemeal" (or whole wheat) loaf will stay fresh for days and makes shaggy crunchy toast. The British influence is apparent in bakery goodies like Eccles buns, sausage rolls, and cream-filled turnovers. "Lamingtons" are a Kiwi specialty—squares of sponge cake dipped in chocolate (or raspberry jell-o) and coconut. Tea biscuits have a whole shelf of their own in every grocery store, and there are dozens of irresistible varieties to sample—apricot dreams, chocolate afghans crunchy with coconut, lemon shortbread, raspberry tartlets—but watch out: they're addictive!

Beer and Wine

Kiwis love their beer, and well they might. There are a number of excellent brands. You have probably already met

Steinlager at home, but there is also Rheineck (a German-type brew), Lion Brown and Lion Red, Speights, and Dominion Breweries Draft Beer (affectionately known as DB, and the social and gastronomical equivalent to our Budweiser). Lion Red became our first choice for its mellow flavor, but we were sorry to learn that it can be found only on the North Island.

Wine-making is a relatively new industry in New Zealand, but in recent years vintners have developed enough sophistication to begin to be taken seriously by world wine experts. The whites are more advanced than the reds, and have a clear, bright quality but without the sharp dryness valued in California wines. Müller-Thurgau is a popular type with Germanic softness. Some bottles we have enjoyed are a crisp Riverlea Select Chablis 1984 from Gisborne, the Montana Marlborough Cabernet Sauvignon 1984 (a well-rounded red with a hint of raspberry), and the full-bodied Villa Maria Chardonnay 1986. Many small wineries are worth investigating; prices start at about NZ$8.00 per bottle. You may also want to try the odd kiwifruit wine just to say you did.

But shopping for beer or wine takes some know-how. You can't just walk into a supermarket and pick up a six-pack. You must look for a "Wholesale Liquor Store," where technically you are supposed to buy at least two gallons (although this rule is not strictly enforced). Or in small towns ask for the "Bottle Store," which is often a separate entrance to the local tavern or pub. (And remember that taverns are closed on Sunday.) A "Wine Shop" will sell no beer except special low-alcohol brands.

Other Beverages

We're sorry to have to say it, but coffee is dreadful in every form in New Zealand. If you absolutely must have your morning cup, bring the makings with you. Otherwise, adapt to the culture and enjoy a pot of fragrant tea.

Tea is such an institution that it has given its name to three meals: morning tea, afternoon tea, and tea. The last-named is an alternative word for dinner. Cafe signs advertising "teas" mean that light, high-carbohydrate meals are served within at any time of day.

Exotic combinations, of natural fruit juices are sold in little boxes and are very refreshing chilled. Try also the bubbly Lemon and Pareroa Water.

RECIPES

RED PEPPER SALAD

1 red bell pepper, seeded and sliced in
    crosswise rings
½ cucumber, peeled, seeded, and cut in
    chunks
3 thin slices of purple onion, divided into
    rings
3 tbsp. oil
1 tbsp. lemon juice
Sprinkle of salt

Combine and toss well.

We find that lettuce crowds the refrigerator, deteriorates quickly, and is hard to wash in a small sink, so our campervan salads tend to raw vegetable improvisations like this.

GRILLED TOMATO-CHEESE SANDWICHES

2 thick slices wholemeal bread
4 tbsp. soft butter
White chedder cheese
2 small tomatoes, sliced

Spread the bread with the butter, then with layers of thinly-sliced cheese. Top with tomatoes and broil until the cheese melts.

A quick and hearty picnic lunch.

COMFORT NOODLES

2 carrots, thinly sliced
4 cups water
1 envelope Maggi chicken noodle soup mix
½ pkg. spiral noodles
Pepper
1 cup cheddar cheese cut in matchsticks or
**   grated**

Boil the carrots in a covered pot until just tender. Add the soup mix, stir well, return to boil, and pour in the noodles. When the noodles are soft, remove the cover for a few minutes over high heat to reduce the sauce to a thin gravy. Off heat, sprinkle with pepper and gently stir in the cheese until it melts throughout.

After a frosty hike on a glacier this is warming and reassuring.

WHITEBAIT FRITTERS

1 egg
1 tbsp. flour
4 tbsp. butter
2 tbsp. oil
Salt and pepper
½ cup whitebait

Beat the egg and flour and seasonings in a bowl, then fold in the whitebait. Heat the oil and butter until frothy and drop in the batter by the spoonful. Flatten and turn when the bottom is lightly browned. Serve with lemon wedges.

JOHN DORY WITH GARLIC AND GINGER

**½ inch green ginger root, shaved very thin or
    grated
3 cloves garlic, minced
2 tbsp. oil
2 fillets of John Dory
Salt and pepper**

Sauté the ginger and garlic in hot oil in a heavy skillet for
30 seconds. Lower the heat a bit and lay the fish in the pan.
In five minutes, turn it carefully with a spatula. Scrape up
the garlic and ginger so it won't burn and heap it on the
fillets. Add salt and pepper to taste. As soon as the fish
flakes, or when it is opaque in the thickest part, it is done.

*This is a classic method of fish preparation from Japan, and the
one that seems to bring out the best in anything that swims.*

SCALLOPS IN WINE-MUSTARD SAUCE

**1 pound scallops
3 tbsp. butter
⅓ cup dry white wine
1 tbsp. mustard
½ pound mushrooms
Salt and pepper**

Pick over the scallops for bits of shell and rinse, drain, and
dry them well. Wipe the mushrooms with a damp paper
towel and cut them in quarters. Heat the butter in a heavy
skillet until it is frothy, then add the scallops and mushrooms. Turn them over constantly for a minute or two, until
the scallops are barely opaque, but before they release their
juices. Mix the mustard and salt and pepper into the wine
and pour it over the scallops for another few seconds until
the sauce is heated through. If this gets away from and you
and turns soupy it can be thickened with a tablespoon of
cornstarch dissolved in a little cold water or you can just eat it
with a spoon.

QUICK LAMB CURRY

2 tbsp. butter
3 cloves garlic, minced
1 pound lean lamb cut for stir-fry (or slice a
      small lamb steak in thin pieces across the
      grain)
½ green pepper, sliced thin
1 onion, minced
1 small apple, cored but unpeeled and sliced
      in eighths
1 tbsp. hot curry powder
¼ cup dry white wine
2 small kumara, cooked and cut in bite-size
      pieces
1 cup frozen green peas
Salt and pepper

Melt the butter in a heavy frying pan and add the garlic. Stir for one minute over high heat. Add lamb and stir until no longer pink. Add green pepper, onion, and apple, lower the heat, and stir in the curry powder, turning the vegetables so they are coated with the spice. Cover the pan and continue cooking until the pepper is barely tender. Add wine if it gets dry. At the end fold in the kumara and frozen peas, heat through, and season with salt and pepper to taste. (If you don't have any leftover kumara, it's okay without.)

CHINESE BEEF AND ASPARAGUS

2 beef "wienersnitzels" without crumbs
4 cloves garlic, minced
1 inch green ginger root, shaved or grated
4 tbsp. oil
3 tbsp. soy sauce
3 tbsp. white wine
⅓ cup water
1 tbsp. cornstarch
1 bunch asparagus
1 bunch green onions

Slice the beef into thin strips and marinate in a sauce made from the soy sauce, wine, and water, and *half* the garlic, ginger, and oil. Wash the asparagus, snap off the tough ends, peel the stalks up two inches from the base, and cut into 3-inch pieces. Wash the green onions, trim off the roots, and cut into 2-inch sections. Heat the reserved oil, garlic, and ginger in a heavy skillet and when it foams, lift the beef out of the marinade and put it in the pan to brown, turning constantly. When all the pink is gone (about one minute), take it out and set it aside. Add more oil if necessary and scrape up the browned bits. Stir-fry the asparagus and onions, tossing constantly, until the asparagus is tender-crisp. Return the beef to the pan, pour in the sauce and stir until thickened.

SILVERBEET WITH BACON

½ bunch silverbeet
1 package (or ½ pound) shoulder bacon
2 or 3 tbsp. butter
3 cloves garlic, minced
1 small onion, sliced

Wash and shred the silverbeet, discarding the stems; set aside. In a heavy skillet fry the bacon in the butter until it is crisp, cutting it into small pieces as it cooks. add more butter if necessary and scrape up the browned bits from the bottom of the pan. Add the garlic and onion; stir and cover. When the onion is tender, add the silverbeet, lower the heat, and replace the cover. Toss frequently until done. Do not add any salt because the bacon has quite enough.

PINEAPPLE AND CAPSICUM-CURRY

2 tbsp. butter
2 cloves garlic, sliced
2 bell peppers (or capsicums) sliced in
    strips—red, yellow, green, and/or black
1 onion, halved and thickly sliced
Salt and pepper
1 tbsp. hot curry powder
1 tomato, sliced
1 wedge fresh pineapple in bite-sized chunks
1 cup water

Sauté the garlic and peppers in the butter for five minutes, then add the onion and cover, but continue to stir frequently. When veges are tender, stir in the curry and salt and pepper, then the tomato and pineapple. Pour in the water and simmer uncovered until the sauce is thick (about 20 minutes).

An offbeat but very tasty accompaniment for those lamb chops.

TAMARILLO SAUCE

6 tamarillos
2 tbsp. oil
1 onion, chopped
1 green pepper
3 tbsp. water
Sugar to taste

Pour boiling water over the tamarillos to loosen their skins, peel and slice them thin. Fry the onion and pepper until soft, add the water and tamarillos, and simmer until blended (about ten minutes). Sweeten to taste and serve as a sauce for lamb or pork.

TAMARILLO CREAM

6 tamarillos
3/4 cup sugar
1 pint heavy cream, whipped

Scald, peel, and slice the tamarillos and simmer eight minutes. Cool. Fold in the sugar, then the whipped cream.

This luscious dessert was served to us by Margaret Johnson when we visited her and her husband Malcolm at their green, green dairy farm on the slopes of Mount Taranaki.

PAVLOVA

Meringue:

> **4 egg whites (6 if the eggs have been re-frigerated)**
> **1 cup sugar**
> **¼ tsp. salt**
> **1 tsp. vinegar**
> **1 tsp. cornstarch**

Filling:

> **1 pint heavy cream, whipped and slightly sweetened**
> **4 kiwifruit, peeled and sliced**
> **¼ cup passionfruit pulp**

Beat the egg whites until they form soft peaks. Sprinkle in the other meringue ingredients gradually, and continue to beat until they are stiff and glossy. Heap in an eight-inch circle or wetted brown paper laid on a baking sheet. Bake at 350 degrees for 15 minutes, or until the meringue rises. Peek, and if all is well, turn off the heat and leave it in the oven for one hour. Cool, and top with whipped cream, kiwifruit, and passionfruit pulp.

This dessert is as Kiwi as food can get. Any kind of fruit can be used. Shirley Jones, who introduced us to Pavlova at a sheep station in Canterbury, fills hers with lemon cream. We realize that you can't accomplish a Pavlova in a motorhome, but someday we all have to bid a reluctant farewell to New Zealand and go home with fond memories and recipes.

CHAPTER 6

Bringing the Kids
(But Not the Dog)

No doubt about it, motorhoming is the way to travel with kids. They have the security of a familiar bed every night, space to play while you're on the road, clean toilets, and the kind of food they're used to. You are spared those excruciating waits in restaurants with tired, cranky little ones, hotel rooms festooned with laundry, and worries about germs in strange bathrooms. Midday naps, potty breaks, and snack times are easily accomplished at a moment's notice by pulling into the next rest area. In the evening you can tuck them in bed, pull the divider curtains, and have a couple of hours of adult time in a way that you never could in a motel.

And New Zealand is a country where people of all ages can have an equally wonderful experience. The things you'll be doing are the active, outdoor things kids love—swimming, boating, hiking, meeting new people, and seeing plants and animals on their own territory. Little children will be entranced with all the sheep, especially if they can pet a lamb, and they'll love the semi-spooky nocturnal houses in zoos. Teenagers can be enticed out of the motorhome by the thrills of whitewater rafting, flightseeing, glacier trekking, and the midway at an A & P show—and you can reassure them that

New Zealand radio plays British and American pop and rock so that they'll know they won't be out of touch with civilization.

But Not the Dog . . .

But the family dog will have to stay at home, much as you'd like to have his enthusiastic company in the fern forest. As we've explained, dogs can be brought into New Zealand only from Australia and the United Kingdom, and then only after a six- to twelve-month stay. Besides, no animal you love should be subjected to a terrifying twelve-hour ride in the baggage compartment.

Planning Ahead

When you reserve your motorhome there are several things to bear in mind for comfort and safety when you're traveling with kids. First, be sure to get a model that is large enough. Elsewhere we've encouraged you to choose the smallest vehicle you can live with, for ease of driving and parking. But unless your child is very small, a pop-top van is probably going to be too snug. Get a four-berth to allow some wiggle room. If you have more than two kids, or they can't share a bed, check on the form of the fifth and sixth beds in the four- to six-berth camper. Sometimes the extra sleeping spaces are hammocks, which are great fun for an older child but might be scary or unsafe for a younger one. The kids will undoubtedly claim the bed over the cab instantly by swarming up the little ladder, but be sure there is a barrier which can be installed at night to keep them from rolling out in their sleep, and don't let them roughhouse up there during the day. It's a long drop to the floor.

Seat Belts

Seat belts are another safety consideration. New Zealand laws about children and car restraints are a bit more lenient than in the U.S., but in general it is required that you and the kids buckle up at all times. If there is a child restraint seat or harness you must use it. If there is none, the child may use an adult seat belt. Young people under 15 are not allowed to travel unrestrained in the front seat unless there is no rear seat or unless all seating positions behind the driver's seat are already occupied by people under 15. Of course you never share a belt with a child or hold him or her on your lap while you're riding. For practical purposes, you'll want to make sure when you reserve your motorhome that there are seat-belts in the back at the table. You don't want to confine the kids on some side bench with zero visibility and no play surface.

What to Pack

If you're renting your motorhome, you won't need to bring along any dishes or linens unless the kids have emotional attachments to a certain cup or blanket. There is one exception: washcloths are not provided because Kiwis consider them a highly personal item. Bring your own. When you pack the toys, a mixture of a few old, familiar things and some new surprises is a wise choice. Choose toys that have lots of play possibilities, like a small doll with interesting changes of clothes and accessories, or a set of small trucks and cars. Spiral-bound drawing pads with colored pencils are good for hours of fun, but don't bring crayons, which melt in the sun. And toys with hundreds of small pieces (Lego is the classic example) can be a constant annoyance in a small living space unless your child is an exceptional picker-upper.

Campgrounds and Kids

When you arrive in a campground you can safely let older kids run, with a few precautions. Make sure they know the route back to "home" from the playground and the toilets. Many camps are large and confusing, and all motorhomes can begin to look alike to a scared and lost child. Most Kiwi motorcamps have trampolines, which kids love but which can be risky for rowdy bouncers. You may want to make some rules about their use. If your kids are new to camping, teach them how to stay on the beaten path and not violate the invisible boundaries of other people's "front yards."

Dividing Up Chores

Kids will feel more a part of the whole enterprise if they have regular tasks on the trip. To help make the morning routine go more quickly, younger children can put dirty clothes in the laundry bag, tie back the curtains, empty the trash, while older kids can unplug and wind up the electrical connection, sweep the floor, and wipe the dew off the windshield. You can even make a game of seeing how quickly you can get on the road after breakfast.

While you're driving, older children and teens can be entrusted with navigating from the map and reading aloud interesting bits from the guidebook, or keeping records of expenditures and computing gas mileage. If you have a surfer aboard he'll tell you emphatically which beaches he wants to visit, but other kids old enough to read the guidebook should also have a democratic hand in deciding which points of interest *they* think they would find of interest.

Sights With High "Kid Appeal"

Actually, we can't think of any of New Zealand's attractions which would *not* appeal to children—except perhaps the opening of Parliament, and you can always promise them ice cream later for good behavior in the upper gallery. Simple things may delight little children the most, like chunking rocks in a lake or watching seagulls from the ferry, while what teenagers like best of all is fast food and other teens, in that order. Nevertheless, here is a brief selection of some places to visit that kids will find particularly great:

The Agrodome: gigantic, curly-horned rams in a stageshow, a fast-talking sheepshearing, and a chance afterward to pet some wooly heads and watch sheep dogs at work. Don't miss the display of native plants and strange moa figures on the forest walk at the end of the parking lot. From Rotorua head around the lake toward Ngongotaha, turn off at Hwy 5. Shows at 9:15 A.M., 11 A.M., and 2:30 P.M.

The Cattledrome: similar show with bovines, plus the opportunity to bottle-feed baby goats and milk a cow by hand. From Queenstown, go 7 km on the road to Coronet Peak and Arrowtown. Shows at 9:30 A.M. and 2:30 P.M.

Maze and Puzzle Centre: an "amazing" 1,500 meters of bridges and passageways for getting lost and found. Puzzle shop, too. Just past Wanaka, north of Queenstown on Hwy 89. A similar but lesser version is in Queenstown at the foot of the gondola.

Kingston Flyer: a quaint and historical little steam-drawn train that makes a one-and-a-quarter hour round trip between Kingston and Fairlight. Departures from Kingston 8:15 A.M., 10 A.M., 11:50 A.M., and 2:30 P.M. 46 km south of Queenstown on Hwy 6.

Kelly Tarlton's Underwater World: a breathtaking journey on a moving walk through an acrylic tunnel under the sea, while manta rays and sharks "fly" just overhead. Auckland, Tamaki Drive by the bay. Open 9 A.M. to 9 P.M.

Merrowvale Model Village: a charming miniature town complete with a tiny working railroad. Sun terrace cafe overlooks the village and serves a fine Devonshire tea. On the road to Waitomo off Hwy 3.

Waitomo Glowworm Caves: a much-touristed but lovely rowboat trip through dark, silent, eerie caves hung with the thousands of tiny lights of glowworms. Motorcamp close by. Hwy 3 south of Hamilton.

"The Signing of the Waitangi Treaty": a dramatic and moving audio-visual account of the passionate all-night debate among the assembled Maori chiefs that led to the signing of a treaty with England. An educational story that will give older kids a strong sense of the dignity of Maori culture. National Park Headquarters, Waitangi National Reserve, Northland. Free. Other National Park audio-visuals are also excellent, especially the volcano show at Tongariro.

The Waihirere Maori Club performing near Rotorua. (Courtesy New Zealand Tourist and Publicity Office)

CHAPTER 7

Letters, Phone Calls, and Other Practical Matters

Every country has its own style of dealing with things like postal service, telephones, and money. It's disconcerting and frustrating to find that you don't know how to buy a stamp, use a public phone, or figure measurements or money. What's more, every country celebrates different holidays, which can cause you problems in planning, scheduling, and keeping beer in the fridge. These tips will help you understand and move with the rhythms of Kiwi life.

MAIL

The post office in New Zealand is a place for mailing letters, but it is also a place for telephoning, paying utility bills, floating a loan and making deposits on a checking account. Consequently, it is sometimes difficult to find the window—or even the building—where they sell the stamps. In smaller towns the post offices are similar to those in small towns at home, with a row of windows labeled as to their function. But in large city post offices, you'll have to ask someone or look for signs.

When you do find the stamp window, a postcard to the

U.S. will require NZ$1.05 in postage. Be sure to mark it "AIR MAIL" conspicuously (ask the clerk for free labels) or it will arrive home after you do. The stamps are beautiful, and you may want to buy a gift packet for a philatelist friend.

Receiving Mail

If you want to receive mail from home while you are on the road, give your friends and relatives a list of the major cities on your itinerary and tell them to address mail to you in care of the post office, like this:

John and Jane Motorhomer
c/o Post Office
Anytown, New Zealand

The post office will hold your mail for one month, and even send it on to your next destination if you ask them.

Telephoning

While you're at the post office, you'll find it's the easiest place from which to make a long distance telephone call, either within New Zealand or overseas. There are directories for most cities and areas of the country, and helpful operators will place your call. The charges are payable in cash only, and the operators keep post office hours: Monday through Friday, 9 A.M. to 5 P.M. You can also make international calls from any phone booth using coins or any U.S. phone charge card, or reversing the charges.

To make a local call from a public phone booth, insert twenty cents, and punch or dial in the number. When your party answers, *immediately* push the button on the *front* of the phone. If your call doesn't go through, push the button on the *side* of the phone for a refund, or use the credit to make another call without reinserting the coins.

When making a long distance call from a private or business phone, dial 010 and ask for "price required." The operator will ring you back after the call is completed and tell you the total charges so you can reimburse the nice person who let you use the phone.

Other useful general numbers:

111—emergency
100—directory assistance (local)
102—directory assistance (long distance)
0172—directory assistance (international)
0170—long distance operator

MONEY

Kiwi money is decimal, and the basic unit is the dollar. The coins are valued at 1, 2, 5, 10, 20, and 50 cents (notice, no quarter).

Travelers' Checks

You can change a little money to tide you over when you arrive at the airport, but the best place for cashing travelers' checks is a bank. If there are several banks from which to choose, it may be worth your while to shop around, as exchange rates differ from one institution to another. Banking hours are Monday through Friday, at least 10 A.M. to 4 P.M., but some banks open as early as 9:00 and some stay open until 4:30 or 5:00. A few in tourist areas even open on Saturday morning. You can also cash a travelers' check at tourist-oriented shops when you make a purchase.

Credit Cards

The most useful credit cards are VISA and Mastercard. You can use them to draw cash at most banks, and they will even work in automatic teller machines if properly encoded. Just ask your issuing bank at home to add a *foreign code* to the card. It will then work not only in New Zealand, but also in Denmark, Sweden, West Germany, Singapore, and South Africa.

Conversion

To make a quick approximate conversion between NZ and U.S. dollars when you're shopping, you should do a preliminary calculation when you change money—and then memorize the result. Take the posted rate (say, 1.38), divide it into 1.00, and you'll come up with .73, the number of U.S. cents equal to a NZ dollar. Then while you're shopping you can bear in mind that NZ$10 equals US$7.30, and figure roughly what each item costs in American money. On large purchases you'll want to use your calculator for an exact figure, but it's a bit gauche to pull it out for every little transaction. Tipping, by the way, is not normally necessary.

METRIC MEASUREMENTS

Like every major country in the world except the U.S. and England (which is changing), New Zealand uses the metric system. For practical purposes, you don't need to memorize all those decimal point equivalencies to function metrically. Just make a mental note that a metre is a bit more than a yard, a kilogram is about two pounds, a kilometre is about 6/10 of a mile, and a litre is about a quart. For more about metres, litres, and miles per gallon, see Chapter 3.

Measuring temperature, however, is a bit trickier, and arithmetic is inevitable. To convert Celsius (centigrade) degrees to Farenheit, multiply by 9, divide by 5, and add 32.

HOLIDAYS

New Zealanders celebrate ten national holidays, many of which are "Monday-ized" whenever possible. These three- and four-day holidays are festive booby traps for the unwary traveler. Plan ahead and make sure you have enough cash, meat, and beer to last until Tuesday. Here are the holidays:

New Year's Day	January 1
Waitangi Day	February 6
Good Friday	
Easter Sunday and Monday	
Anzac Day	April 25
Queen's Birthday	First Monday in June

Labour Day	Fourth Monday in October
Christmas Day	December 25
Boxing Day	December 26

In addition, each province has its own anniversary celebration. Expect heavier-than-normal traffic during holiday weekends, as Kiwis like to hit the road just like we do.

A sampling of New Zealand's exotic fruits. (Photo by David Shore)

CHAPTER 8

Staying Safe and Healthy

We Americans tend to be extremely security-conscious—maybe because we watch so much violent television, or maybe because so many of us live in or near crowded cities where violent crime is a daily reality. Happily, when you're in New Zealand you can ease up a little on those fears. This is a safe country, although Kiwis, not to be outdone by overseas visitors, will try hard to convince you that *their* city crime statistics are getting to be as bad as anybody else's.

Security Basics

You're perfectly secure walking together on city streets or remote trails, and sleeping in your motorhome in a campground or a rest area. But there are some basic precautions that all travelers anywhere should observe as a matter of course. It probably isn't always necessary, but we feel better if we lock our vehicle when we go away from it for any length of time, even in the campground. We also take care not to leave cameras and other valuables in plain sight while we're gone. (Although we saw a pair of motorcycles parked by the road whose Kiwi owners had gone off for a hike and left their helmets *and leather jackets* draped over the handlebars without a qualm.) It's just not smart for women to walk alone in dark places, or to hang a purse over the back of the chair in a crowded cafe. Nor is it wise to put temptation in somebody else's way by leaving your purse or daypack hanging outside the stall when you shower or lying unattended on the beach while you swim. Zip up your purse between purchases when you're shopping; keep your wallet in an inside or secure pocket in crowds. Divide your money, credit cards, and traveler's checks among the two of you and a hiding place in the camper, and have an extra set of motorhome keys made. In other words, use common sense—and then relax.

Health Basics

New Zealand is a healthful environment as well as a safe one. The lack of population pressures means a lack of pollution from smoke, chemicals, and noise. Kiwis are extremely respectful of their beautiful landscape and they are careful to preserve the ecology unsullied. Locally produced food is fresher, more nutritious, and needs no preservatives. The pace is unhurried, the style casual, the people genial. You'll find yourself breathing deeply of the cool, clean air and letting go of anxieties and tensions.

But again, certain precautions should be part of any traveler's bag of tricks. We take 1,000 miligrams a day of Vitamin C on the road, and we've noticed that the only time we ever get sick on a trip is when we run out. It's important to go easy the first couple of times you sample a new fruit or seafood in New Zealand, in case of an allergic reaction. Getting enough exercise is gloriously pleasant here, but be sure the magnificent scenery doesn't tempt you to hours and hours of sedentary windshield-viewing without at least stopping occasionally for a stroll in the forest or a turn around a village square.

The changeability of the weather can be a health problem and dressing in layers is the solution. A frosty morning can blossom into a tropical noon, followed in half an hour by glowering clouds and pouring rain. When you go off hiking or boating, don't trust those smiling skies: always carry a sweater and a lightweight rain poncho in your daypack.

Adjusting for Time Change

Jet lag is not a serious health hazard, but it can be disorienting for the first three or four days. Recently a number of articles and books have offered elaborate schemes for overcoming the effects, mostly by turning your life upside-down for a week before you leave. We find all this more trouble than it's worth. In New Zealand jet lag is not as bad as you might expect, given the great distance of the flight. Actually, your body is only four hours out of sync, and a journey southwest, for some reason, is far less stressful than one in the opposite direction. It helps to know that the exhaustion, loss of appetite, and feelings of unreality that you're experiencing are normal and temporary. Just take it easy at first. Don't force yourself to eat, take naps only when you must, and try to get into the new diurnal rhythm as soon as you can. Treat yourself to a motel with a jacuzzi the first night, and then go straight to a nearby motorcamp for a day or two. Don't launch into strenuous sightseeing or driving immediately. Leave time in your itinerary for your body to adjust.

Sandflies

Eden had its serpent, and New Zealand has sandflies. Presumably the Creator put them in Kiwiland to remind us that this earthly paradise is not quite as good as the heavenly one to follow. These tiny vicious insects are unbelievably persistent and their bites itch horribly for days and days. Don't wait until you notice them sitting on your arm—it's already too late at that point. Before you go outdoors protect yourself with insect repellent on every inch of exposed skin. DEET is effective, or any product containing N-diethyltoluamide.

Fire Safety

Inside your motorhome we want to warn you to be super-careful with fire. We speak from experience. When we were novice vanners, we used to think it was romantic to have candlelit dinners—until the night David leaned across the table for a kiss and sat back with his hair in a crown of flames. From the candle, not the kiss. Luckily, we got the fire smothered before he was burned, but ever since we have been very aware of fire safety. Please be sure to tie your curtains well away from the stove when you are cooking, and be careful not to let hot fat ignite in the broiler. Always open the window a bit when you cook to prevent carbon monoxide buildup, and never use the stove for heat while you sleep.

Doctors and Medicine

In New Zealand medical care is high quality and very inexpensive by American standards. A visit to a doctor's office (or his "surgery") cost us $12NZ in 1988. Prescription drugs are government-subsidized and free except for a one dollar handling charge. Prescriptions can be filled and other medicines bought at the "chemist's," which is like an American mini-drugstore. Every large town will have at least one "urgent chemist," or after-hours pharmacy. If you should be injured in an accident of any kind (God forbid) the government will reimburse you for all medical costs.

However, it is still a good idea to cheek with your U.S. medical insurer before you leave to find out their rules for overseas reimbursement. Kaiser Permanente, for instance, will pay only on life-threatening emergencies, and you must notify them within 48 hours of the occurence.

If you are at all prone to hay fever or asthma, be sure to take your medication with you. The population of New Zealand has a puzzling and astronomically high rate of respiratory allergies, and it is possible that you may find yourself reacting to unfamiliar pollens or whatever it is that makes so many Kiwis wheeze.

Campervan Mental Health

Living together happily in a motorhome or van draws on all the skills of maintaining a good relationship, but on an intensified level. For your mental health, use the techniques we have outlined in Chapter 4 under "Campervan choreography." Be aware of the other person's need for space, both physical and psychological, and give a bit more than you think your partner needs. The taller vanmate should be careful not to sprawl out all over the seat so that the other person has to curl up in a cramped corner. Watch out for irritating habits in yourself—tapping, whistling, hair-twirling. These can escalate at close quarters into major annoyances. And more assertive people should be careful not to thoughtlessly impose their preferences about music, radio programs, and bedtime on gentler partners. Discussion and compromise are important tools, and a willingness to speak up as soon as something bothers you. All this is excellent practice for general compatibility as well as happy motorhome living, and you may go home with your relationship in better shape than when you arrived.

Spinning wool during a farm stay. (Photo by David Shore)

CHAPTER 9

Beyond Sightseeing
Pursuing Your Sporting Enthusiasms

Picture yourself shooting for a hole-in-one from the base of a smoldering volcano, or casting your line out into a roaring river full of rainbow trout. Or heliskiing down an Alpine glacier with sparkling peaks towering all around (in July!). Or flying among those peaks. Or climbing them.

Kiwis are avid outdoors enthusiasts, and it's easy to see why. Just about anything you can do anywhere else is better in New Zealand. Clean air and water, beautiful scenery and plenty of wide open spaces make this an outdoor paradise. From birdwatching to jetboating, you won't be bored here.

Golf

Golf is very popular, and you're never far from a course. Be it a municipal or private golf club, most feature challenging designs, scenic locations and high-quality support facilities. Private clubs welcome visitors from affiliated clubs in other countries. A letter of introduction from your home club is advisable. In high season (summer), it's a good idea to notify them in advance of your intended visit.

You don't need to drag your clubs across the Pacific; most

courses will rent or sell you everything you need. Greens fees range from about NZ$10 to NZ$25.

The Air New Zealand Shell Open, the country's biggest golf event, is held in late November at Titirangi, a beautiful mountaintop course. In December, there's the New Zealand Open and the NZ PGA tournament. There are also pro-am tournaments scheduled in February and March.

For a complete listing of the more than 400 golf courses and other information, contact the New Zealand Golf Association, P.O. Box 11842, Wellington.

Tennis

If you're a tennis nut, you're in luck. New Zealand is full of people like you, and there are tennis courts in every city and town. Bring your own racquet or rent one there. Court charges range from free to NZ$5 per hour for outdoor courts, to NZ$20 per hour for indoor, usually payable in honesty boxes.

You can choose from grass, astroturf, or clay courts, and you can even arrange matches with Kiwi players by writing in advance to the New Zealand Lawn Tennis Association, P.O. Box 11541, Wellington. They can also provide a listing of public courts all over the country. Local public relations offices also have that information.

Fishing

New Zealand is well-known around the world as a great place to fish, whether you're going after a 10-pound rainbow trout or a 600-pound blue marlin. The lakes and rivers are well-stocked with rainbow and brown trout, which have flourished here since being introduced nearly 100 years ago. They are large and feisty, so you'll need a stiff action medium-weight rod and a reel holding 100 yards of backing.

Trout season is October through April except for Lake Taupo, Lake Rotorua, and the southern lakes, where it's all year 'round. Chinook salmon run in January, February, and March. A license is required for trout fishing. A special one-month visitor's license is available for NZ$55 for adults, NZ$11 or children. You can also get a daily or week-long local license at a sports shop.

Big game fishing is best on the east coast of the North Island. There you'll find marlin, shark, yellowtail, swordfish, and tuna. No license is required. For more information, contact your nearest NZTP office.

Sailing

No visit to the "City of Sails" would be complete without a boat ride, and Auckland, home of the former America's Cup yacht *New Zealand,* has a harbor full of boats of all sizes and shapes available for hire. There are also boat rental operations at the Bay of Islands, Bay of Plenty, Coromandel Peninsula, Lake Taupo, and Wellington on the North Island, and the Marlborough Sounds, Te Anau, Fiordland, Nelson, Lake Benmore, Lake Manapouri, and Lyttelton Harbour on the South Island.

If you plan to be in New Zealand in the summer (November through February), it may be wise to book in advance for the more popular venues of the Bay of Islands, the Hauraki Gulf (Auckland), and the Marlborough Sounds. The other locations and times of the year present no problems.

You can rent a "bareboat" (sail it yourself), a "skipper-charter" (full crew, including cook), or take a cruise with a group. Motorboats are available in all sizes, as are sailboats. If you're bareboating, you can join a flotilla with other boats, led by an experienced skipper who can show you some interesting islands, beaches, and fishing and diving locations, as well as navigational tips for the area.

For more information, contact the NZTP.

Surfing and Windsurfing

Water and wind are two things New Zealand has in plenty, and there's ample opportunity to harness their power here. The waves are biggest on the west coast, and Raglan is world-famous for its long break. Muriwai, north of Auckland, is a favored venue for national surfing competitions, and New Plymouth on the Taranaki coast is very popular. On the east coast there is the Coromandel Peninsula, Gisborne, Wellington, Christchurch, and Dunedin, with more gentle waves. Matakuna Island and Great Barrier Island are popular, but you must reach them by boat. To find the surfing spot that that's best for you, contact the New Zealand Surfriders Association, P.O. Box 737, New Plymouth.

Windsurfing has become very popular here, with Kiwi equipment competing with the world's best. You're never far from a breezy lake, beach, or bay, and winds can vary from 15 knots all the way up to 40 around the lower North Island.

There are windsurfing schools throughout the country, so even beginners can try it. For information contact the New Zealand Boardsailing Association, P.O. Box 37213, Parnell, Auckland.

Jet Boating

This popular activity is 100 percent home-grown, and the Kiwis do it best. The jet boat was invented in New Zealand for use on its shallow rivers. It has no propeller to snag on the bottom, but uses a jet propulsion unit powered by a big engine to shoot water through high-pressure stern nozzles. This propels the boat over rapids and around rocks at up to 50 mph. It's not for the faint of heart, or for those who don't like to get wet. If roller coasters bore you, try this.

You'll find lots of jet boat operators in Queenstown. For a complete list, contact the NZTP.

Rafting

Another white-knuckle whitewater sport is rafting on New Zealand's wild and scenic rivers. Trips can run from one hour to five days, and usually include periods of leisurely paddling through quiet stretches of water, watching the scenery float by. The NZTP can give you a list of rafting operators.

Jet boating on the Shotover River near Queenstown. (Courtesy New Zealand Tourist and Publicity Office)

Canoeing

New Zealand has more than 1,000 canoeable rivers, as well as lakes and harbors. Canoes are available for rent in many locations, and you can enjoy flatwater sightseeing or whitewater, graded by degree of difficulty.

For further information, contact the NZ Canoeing Association, P.O. Box 5125, Auckland.

Diving

Jacques Cousteau loves New Zealand, and it's easy to see why. One of the world's five best underwater photographic sites is here. But great diving is not limited to one site; crystal clear waters and colorful fish and plant life are found in many places around the coastline, near offshore islands and even in volcanic crater lakes.

But you can enjoy New Zealand's underwater glories without even getting wet. Kelly Tarlton's Underwater World in Auckland lets the fish do the diving while you stroll through a clear acrylic tunnel beneath the harbor. Sharks, manta rays, and all kinds of ocean fish come within inches of you in complete safety. It's a truly unique experience, invented and developed by a Kiwi diver who wanted everyone to experience the wonders of the deep.

But getting back to actual diving, the Poor Knight Islands are the venue of that world-class photogenic site. Drop-offs, caves, arches, and lots of beautiful fish make this the most popular diving spot. But there are others.

The Three Kings Islands, floating northwest of Cape Reinga are the site of an old shipwreck. Large and interesting fish are reportedly seen there. But the islands are a long way offshore, and more difficult to get to than other good spots like the Bay of Islands, White Island, and many other east coast locations.

More shipwrecks can be found around Great Barrier Island, off the Coromandel Peninsula, and it's a lot easier to get to than the Three Kings. But there's no scuba diving allowed; it's snorkeling only at Great Barrier.

Scuba gear can be easily rented all over the country, so don't bother lugging your tanks and wetsuit along. Summer and fall (February to June) are best for visibility. It often ranges up to 200 feet in that season. In spring (October-December), however, the plankton bloom cuts visibility sharply.

If you have a diver's identity certificate, bring it. For more information, contact the New Zealand Underwater Association, P.O. Box 875, Auckland 1. Your NZTP office can give you an up-to-date list of dive charter boats.

Hiking

They call it tramping here, and you do it on a track, not a trail. It's a wonderful way to see New Zealand's unusual flora and fauna close-up. Start walking through a lush native rain forest full of ferns and mossy trees, and you're in another world. Beautiful friendly birds flit around you, chattering their welcome. You'll cross gurgling creeks and discover roaring waterfalls. The track may end at a beach on a secluded lake where you can jump in for a cooling swim and spread out your lunch on the picnic table.

New Zealand has 10 national parks and 21 forest parks, each with many different tracks. The more famous ones are the Milford, Hollyford, Routeburn, and Heaphy Tracks. Most tracks are signposted as to length in distance and time, as well as degree of difficulty. December through April is the best time to tramp. Wear layered clothes and carry a little fold-up raincoat or poncho. Weather conditions can change abruptly. Good walking shoes are a must, too; you may encounter slippery places or rocks to climb over.

Don't worry about snakes; there are none in New Zealand. There *are* sandflies, however, little black things whose bite makes you itch for days. We strongly recommend insect repellent like DEET, Autan, or Black Flag Stick, which are available in New Zealand.

Don't forget, "exotic forest" means pine trees there, while their "native bush" is exotic to us.

For more information, write the New Zealand Walkways Commission, c/o Department of Conservation, Private Bag, Wellington or the New Zealand Forest Service, Private Bag, Wellington.

Mountaineering

If you're a mountain climber, you've got a challenge ahead of you. There are 30 peaks in New Zealand higher than 9,000 feet, all topped by Mt. Cook at over 12,000. You may have seen higher mountains, but the Southern Alps are so steep and sharp, they are not to be taken lightly. The unpredictable and often severe weather adds even greater challenge.

Climbing is best between December and March, but some climbers prefer the extended winter calm periods. There are quite a few huts, most maintained by the national parks that surround all of New Zealand's big peaks. These huts are equipped with kerosene stoves, first aid kits, bunks with bedding, and even radios for safety checks with park headquarters. And you can rent or buy climbing equipment in many locations throughout the country.

For more information, contact the NZ Mountain Guides Association, P.O. Box 20, Mt. Cook.

Running

Kiwis love to run (especially the larger, beakless species), and if you do, too, you'll have plenty to do and see in New Zealand. The fresh air and beautiful scenery of the countryside are perfect for a jog whenever you feel like it. You can always park your motorhome at a rest area or motor camp and take off up the road.

For more organized running, New Zealand schedules many events throughout the country, mostly from November through May. NZTP can give you a schedule of events for the time you'll be there. The Round The Bays Run in March is billed as the world's largest fun run. Tens of thousands of runners pound the pavement around Auckland's waterfront, from Victoria Park to St. Heliers.

Triathlon fans will find all they can handle here, too. Events are scheduled nearly every weekend from October through April. New Zealand's mountains, rivers, and lakes inspire multisport events which include cross-country running, canoeing, and skiing, in addition to normal triathlon sports.

For more information on running, contact the NZ Amateur Athletic Association, P.O. Box 741, Wellington. For triathlons, it's the NZ Triathlon Association, P.O. Box 33444, Takapuna.

Skiing

The "Land of the Long White Cloud" was named for its unbroken line of snow-capped mountains. New Zealand is a skier's paradise, with some of the best ski fields in the world. In winter you can ski on both the North and South Islands, from the slopes of an active volcano to the scenic wonders of a glacier. There are about 20 recognized skiing areas, most relatively inexpensive, ranging from commercial ski fields to club fields. Heliskiing and cross-country skiing are becoming very popular, as is glacier ski-touring. Mount Cook Line runs a Tasman Glacier ski tour with an Alpine guide who leads you through ice caves and other fascinating features. You can contact them at (800) 478-2665.

Ski season on the North Island runs from mid-July through October; on the South Island it starts in early July and ends in late September. Weather conditions often extend the season, however. The NZTP can provide you with a list of ski areas and other information.

Flightseeing

Airplanes, helicopters, hot-air balloons, gliders, and even hang gliders are available all over New Zealand, and they add a special dimension to the country's spectacular scenery.

The ski plane, which can take off and land on snow as well as on a normal runway, was invented here for Mount Cook Line, which has exclusive landing rights on the glaciers of the Southern Alps. Ski plane flights are not cheap, but they're worth it.

Other flights, some run by other lines, take you out over places like Milford Sound, the Bay of Islands, volcanic White Island, Rotorua's thermal area, Queenstown, and just about everywhere else.

Flights are often booked up well in advance in high season, and it's a good idea to do the same. Your travel agent or the NZTP can help you with that.

Hot air ballooning is another way to see the sights. You can catch one in Queenstown. There are gliding schools based in Twizel near Mt. Cook, and hang gliding is best on the west coast beach of Muriwai, north of Auckland, and at Queenstown. You can get the feel of hang gliding without risk with the world's first hang gliding simulator. It's a hang glider towed behind a speedboat in Auckland. For information on that, contact the NZ Hang Gliding Association, 11B McVay St., Napier.

Horseriding

There are places where your motorhome just can't go, and and one alternative is horse-trekking. There are guided trail rides in many parts of New Zealand, or you can just rent a horse for a day or more and head out on your own. Even beginners will find the well-trained horses easy to handle, and the guides ride ahead of and behind the party, keeping everything safe and under control. It's an interesting way to see the countryside.

For a list of horseriding operators, see the NZTP.

Horse Racing

If you're a true racing fan, you probably know that some of the world's best thoroughbreds are bred in New Zealand. Horse racing is one of the country's top spectator sports, with

260 race meetings held throughout the year. There are major tracks all over New Zealand, and you're bound to catch a race during your visit.

Harness racing is also popular here. Races are usually run at night under lights. If you ask the average sporting Kiwi what's important in life, he'll probably echo the traditional answer (with tongue in cheek): "Rugby, Racing, and Beer."

For more information, including a schedule of race meetings, contact the NZTP.

Rugby

Rugby is English-style football, and it's New Zealand's national winter sport. It's played all over the country on weekends and holidays from June through September, and you can usually find a game to attend if you're there during that time. The more important games require seat reservations, just like at home.

Cricket

Cricket is the favorite summer sport. It's similar to baseball, and it's usually played on Saturdays and holidays from November through April. Cricket is a strictly amateur game here.

Birdwatching

Bring your binoculars; there are some fascinating birds here! Even those who don't call themselves birdwatchers will get a kick out of the strange and genuinely entertaining birds flying (and walking) around New Zealand.

Floating out in the South Pacific, nearly 1,000 miles from its closest neighbor, New Zealand has many native species that developed without any outside interference. Originally, there were no mammalian predators, so many birds gave up the power of flight. The predators arrived with the people, who also cleared a lot of vegetation. These and other factors resulted in the extinction or near-extinction of many species. The Moa, a giant flightless bird standing up to 13 feet tall, was hunted to extinction by the first human inhabitants, known only as the Moa Hunters.

But there are nearly 300 species of birds still to be seen and enjoyed. Kiwis are nocturnal and therefore hard to spot in the wild, but you can see them in Kiwi exhibit houses, located in tourist areas throughout the country. The Takahe, our personal favorite, is one of the rarest birds here. There are only 120 of them. They can be seen at the Te Anau Wildlife Center and in Wairarapa.

The Fantail will find you if you walk through a forest. This friendly little bird flits all around you, chirping merrily. You will hear the Bellbird, whose call resembles a very sophisticated set of door chimes. The Tui sounds similar, but stronger and coarser. The parrot-like Kea is the clown of the group, swaggering right up to tourists to have its picture taken.

There are many other fascinating birds here. For more information, contact the Royal Forest and Bird Protection Society of New Zealand, 26 Brandon St., Wellington. For information on birdwatching tours, contact the World Wildlife Fund, 22 Brandon St., Wellington.

Farm Stays

New Zealand is an agricultural country, and to really experience it you must spend some time on a farm. The country's 70 million sheep are a vital part of the economy and the lifestyle, and to leave them out would be like avoiding wine in France or coffee in Brazil. The dairy industry is also very large and important here.

But the best thing about a farm stay is meeting the people. Farmers have long been the aristocracy here, and Kiwis are gracious hosts. They make you feel so at home, it's like visiting old friends on their country estate. Sitting around the fire in the evening, chatting about life in general, learning to spin wool, and then sitting down to a hearty farm dinner, you feel like one of the family. Your accommodation is often the spare bedroom. And after riding around the farm and watching the dogs work with the sheep, you begin to understand Kiwi farm life.

Farm stays can be booked in advance through travel agents and wholesalers or spontaneously through a local registry. Inquire at NZTP for information. Often you can just drive up to the main house on an interesting farm and ask.

Photography

It's hard to take a bad picture in New Zealand. With all that magnificent scenery, you could almost stick your camera out the window and click the shutter at random and still bring home a great set of photos.

Even so, we decided that a few tips from the experts wouldn't hurt. Since most professional and amateur photographers prefer Kodak films, we spoke to Kodak New Zealand about photography down under. They told us that film manufactured there is different from that obtainable in North America. It's specially calibrated for the brilliant South Pacific light, and gives much better results than film you might bring from home. It seems more expensive to buy it there, but the price usually includes processing (check for this information on the outside of the package). As tourism and demand increase, Kodak is selling more film without processing to make the price more competitive.

For color prints, the fine-grained Kodacolor Gold is quite popular in ISO 100 and 200 speeds. For top-quality slides, however, we stick to Kodachrome. It's the best we've found for crisp color separation and good saturation. We prefer ISO 64. A skylight or UV filter enhances these qualities even more, compensating for the higher ultraviolet light in New Zealand. Autofocus cameras take sharp photos and leave you more time to enjoy your subject firsthand.

New Zealand
NORTH ISLAND

Spirits Bay
North Cape
Cape Reinga
Cape Karikari
Ninety-Mile Beach
Bay of Islands
Cape Brett
Kaitaia
Kerikeri
Waitangi
Paihia
Kaikohe
Hokianga Harbour
Whangarei
Hen & Chicken Islands
Little Barrier Is.
Great Barrier Is.
Kaipara Harbour
Hauraki Gulf
Coromandel Peninsula
Coromandel
AUCKLAND
Papakura
Thames
Pukekohe
Paeroa
Waiuku
Bay of Plenty
Huntly
L. Waikare
Mt. Maunganui
White Is.
Ngaruawahia
Tauranga
Cape Runaway
Hamilton
Matamata
Whakatane
Cambridge
L. Rotorua
Waitomo Caves
ROTORUA
L. Tarawera
Te Kuiti
Mangakino
Atiamuri
Murupara
Mokau R.
Wairakei
Gisborne
Taupo
Taupo
L. Waikaremoana
New Plymouth
Tokaanu
Turangi
Motuka R.C.
Cape Egmont
Chateau Tongariro
Tongariro
1968m 6458'
Wairoa
Mt. Egmont
2517m 8260'
Mt. Ruapehu
Mt. Ngauruhoe
2796m 9175'
2290m 7503'
Poverty
Stratford
Ohakune
Mahia Pe
Hawera
Waiouru
Hawke Bay
Patea
Napier
Hastings
Wanganui R.
Taihape
Mangaweka
Cape Kidnappers
WANGANUI
Marton
Feilding
Waipukurau
Rangitikei R.
Dannevirke
Cape Farewell
Palmerston North
Woodville
Manawatu R.
Pahiatua
Farewell Spit
Golden Bay
Levin
Cape Turnagain
Tasman Bay
Kapiti Is.
Takaka
Paraparaumu
Karamea
Motueka
Masterton
Nelson
Picton
L. Wairarapa
Buller R.
WELLINGTON
Blenheim
Westport
Murchison
L. Rotoiti
Palliser Bay
Inangahua
Junction
Mt. Travers
2338m 7671'
KAIKOURA Ra.
COOK STRAIT
Cape Palliser
Reefton
Clarence R.

N

Courtesy Air New Zealand

CHAPTER 10

The Way We Went
A Suggested First-Trip Itinerary

Whenever we talk to other travelers who have been to New Zealand, we hear what seems to be an echo of our own feelings after our first trip: "We wish we had more time!" "There's so much to see!" "We have to go back!"

Somehow New Zealand is much bigger on the inside than it is on the outside. Once you start driving and taking in all the spectacular sights and unforgettable experiences, you'll see what we mean.

But one of the nice things about all of this bigness is that it's relatively compact. You can get from one place to another fairly quickly over the smooth, lightly-traveled roads, or you can amble along at a leisurely pace, stopping often and enjoying the finer points. We like to explore interesting side roads, small towns, roadside fruit stands, highway rest areas and Devonshire tearooms. There is such a wealth of things to experience, it's almost impossible not to have a fascinating trip, wherever you go.

OUR TRIP

On our first trip we wanted to see everything, of course, and from our experiences in Europe we thought a month

New Zealand
SOUTH ISLAND

Cape Farewell
Farewell Spit
Golden Bay
Tasman Bay
Takaka
Karamea
Motueka
Nelson
Bl
Buller R.
Cape Foulwind
Westport
Murchison
L. Rotoiti
Inangahua
Junction
L. Rotoroa
Mt. Travers
2338m 7671
KAIKOURA Ra.
Reefton
Clare
Springs Junction
Mt. Tapuaenuku 28
Kaikoura
Greymouth
Grey R.
Hochstetter
Hanmer Springs
Hokitika
L. Kaniere
L. Brunner
Waiau R.
Cheviot
Otira
Arthur's Pass
Hurunui R.
Ross
Mt. Murchison
2199m 7873
Waipara
Imberley
Harihari
L. Coleridge
Rangiora
Pegasus Bay
Malte Brun 3176m 10,421
Waimakariri R.
Franz Josef Glacier
Fox Glacier
Mt. Hutt 2188m 780
CHRISTCHURCH
MOUNT COOK
9764m
Mt. Tasman
3497m 11,475
Methven
Rolleston
Lyttelton
Bruce Bay
32,349
MOUNT
COOK
Akaroa
Jackson Bay
Mt. Sefton
3157m 10,359
Haa
L. Tekapo
Ashburton
Ellesmere
Fairlie
Rakaia R.
Mt. Aspiring
3036m 9957
L. Ohau
L. Pukaki
Geraldine
Rangitata R.
L. Wanaka
Omarama
Temuka
Milford Sound
Mt. Earnslaw
Mt. Hawea
Timaru
Sutherland Falls
Coronet Peak
Wanaka
Lindis Pass
Benmore
Bligh Sound
Mitre Peak
1446m 5413
Cardrona
Waimate
George Sound
Arrowtown
QUEENSTOWN
Cromwell
Waitaki R.
L. Wakatipu
Damaru
MILFORD
REMARKABLES
Alexandra
Te
EYRE Mts.
Roxburgh
TE ANAU
Mossburn
L. Manapouri
Five Rivers
Lawrence
DUNEDIN
Manapouri
L. Monowai
L. Hauroko
Gore
Taieri R.
Milton
Clinton
Clutha R.
Edendale
INVERCARGILL
Bluff
FOVEAUX STRAIT
Mataura R.
Paterson
Inlet
Oban
Mason Bay
Stewart Island

N

Courtesy Air New Zealand

would be plenty of time for one country. We were wrong.
True, you can get around to many of the major sights and
attractions in a short time, but driving a motorhome lets you
see everything in between. Once you get a glimpse of the
everyday life and people of the country, you can't help wanting to see more. And once you find that perfect beach, fishing lake, fern forest, or ski run, you can't help wanting to stay
there just a bit longer.

But to fit everything you want to see and do into a certain
length of time, you must make choices. Take a look at the
itinerary of our first trip. It should give you a rough idea of
how far you can go and what you can do in one day. We've
given distances and approximate driving times (exclusive of
stops). Use it to plan your own itinerary.

Day 1—Arrive Auckland

Our motorhome was waiting at the airport, and the driver
took us back to the depot to sign papers and receive a brief-
ing on how to use all the little gadgets. They also gave us
directions to the nearby Oakwood Manor Motor Hotel.

We drove directly there, as it was already late afternoon
and we were tired from the flight. There was a spa pool in
our room, and after a few restoring dips, we got our second
wind and headed for town. We used public transport (pleasant and interesting), not wanting to get used to right-hand
drive in New Zealand's largest city at night. Kelly Tarlton's
Underwater World was a great experience, and the attached
restaurant was clean and pleasant, with a nice harbor view.
We took a taxi back. It was not overly expensive and the
driver, a cheerful woman, didn't expect a tip (hardly any
Kiwi does).

Day 2—Still in Auckland

Auckland is a beautiful city full of interesting things to see
and do, so we drove up to the North Shore suburb of Takapuna and parked at the Takapuna Beach Motor Camp. It's

a nice place, if a bit pricey. We took a bus into town and picked up a copy of the *Tourist Times,* a newspaper that tells of all the attractions available to visitors. You can choose from harbor cruises, museums, the zoo, free guided walks, sporting events, theatre, ballet, and lots of things for the kids. We took the ferry back across the harbor to the delightful suburb of Devonport, (NZ$2.00 each). It was a lovely ride, with picturesque city views and sailboats everywhere. We took a short bus ride back to Takapuna.

NORTH ISLAND
Approximate Kilometers

```
170 302 660 454 202 206 280 234 241 369 330 423 325 127 504 | AUCKLAND
674 202 550 468 437 298 350 287 745 599 432 216 829 394 | GISBORNE
297 192 533 327  75 107 153 107 368 242 203 296 452 | HAMILTON
155 627 983 779 527 531 605 561 108 694 555 748 | KAITAIA
593 310 334 252 307 143 311 225 664 412 244 | NAPIER
500 268 317 122 159 269  98 183 571 222 | NATIONAL PARK
539 397 355 160 183 398 296 312 610 | NEW PLYMOUTH
 71 543 901 695 164 447 521 475 | PAIHIA
404  85 462 305 150  86  82 | ROTORUA
450 167 380 223 223 168 | TAUPO
376  96 548 391 151 | TAURANGA
372 235 463 268 | WAITOMO CAVES
624 390 195 | WANGANUI
819 547 | WELLINGTON
472 | WHAKATANE
WHANGAREI
```

```
                                                                WESTPORT
                                                        WANAKA  467
                                                 TIMARU 273 497
                                         TE ANAU 489 273 840
                              QUEENSTOWN  170 335 117 684
                                  PICTON  826 992 503 764 288
                           NELSON  110  873 1029 591 756 226
                  MOUNT COOK  759 671 328 484 211 211 664
         MILFORD SOUND  550 1150 1113 291 121 610 394 961
      INVERCARGILL  278 444 1007 919 187 157 416 278 855
             HAAST  433 539 356 611 673 262 418 418 145 422
        GREYMOUTH  321 754 860 510 290 352 583 739 350 466 101
      FRANZ JOSEF  179 142 575 769 498 469 579 404 560 493 287 280
         DUNEDIN  563 742 421 217 411 331 790 702 283 290 199 276 695
   CHRISTCHURCH  362 427 248 738 579 773 331 428 340 486 652 163 424 333
      BLENHEIM  312 674 503 324 645 891 085 643 116  28 798 964 475 736 260
  ARTHURS PASS  440 150 451 241  98 383 668 922 412 388 468 645 801 252 383 199
```

SOUTH ISLAND
Approximate Kilometers

Day 3—Auckland to Bay of Islands (238 km, 3 hrs.)

Rolling up the Hibiscus Coast via State Highway (S.H.) 1, we were oohing and aahing the whole way. We stopped at Waiwera, a lovely little seaside resort whose name is Maori for "hot water." It's appropriately named, for there they have thermal swimming pools, a "swim-in" theatre where you can soak while watching the big screen, and the "Chutes and Choobs," the world's wildest waterslides. Down the road there's a beautiful beach.

From there we continued north around Whangarei Harbour and on to the Bay of Islands, a subtropical paradise and the venue of the Treaty of Waitangi, which established New Zealand as a British commonwealth. We toured the Treaty House, walked around the beautiful grounds and through the fern forest, and watched a very well-produced, informative and moving audiovisual presentation that gives a perspective on the events that laid the foundation of Maori/European relations. There are also boat trips, water sports, and white-sand beaches.

There's a motor camp near the beach, but we turned inland on Puketona Road (3 km) to the Old Wharf Road, where we found the Falls Motor Inn and Caravan Park. This is an idyllic motor camp on the Waitangi River with a view of Haruru Falls. We parked on a little peninsula shaded by a royal palm, and in the evening we luxuriated in the spa pool and gazed dreamily at the floodlit falls. Patty cooked up a tasty lamb chop dinner, after which we slept well.

Day 4—Bay of Islands to Doubtless Bay (87 km, 1½ hrs.)

We took Provincial Highway (P.H.) 10 north out of Pakaraka and drove through rolling green countryside up to Doubtless Bay, reportedly named by Captain Cook who said it was "doubtless a bay." He was right. It's a wonderful bay,

Hungry ducks in a motor camp. (Photo by David Shore)

Haruru Falls. (Photo by David Shore)

with a nice roadside rest area where we parked and walked the exquisite curve of beach, ringed by lush grass and big trees with gnarled horizontal branches perfect for lazy climbing and watching the long, slow waves and the peaks of the offshore islands. After a swim in the warm, clear water, we had dinner and enjoyed the cool, quiet evening. The rest area was a perfect spot for freecamping.

Day 5—Doubtless Bay to Kohukohu (67 km, 1½ hrs.)

We followed P.H. 10 until it ended at S.H. 1 and turned south to Kaitaia, a nice town settled by Dalmatian gum diggers. Bus tours of Ninety Mile Beach leave from Mount Cook Line (phone 575), or Star Mini Tours (phone 724), both on Commerce Street, every day at 9:00 A.M. They go all the way to Cape Reinga, the northernmost tip of New Zealand, and return at 5:00 P.M.

It's unsafe and unwise to try to drive the beach yourself, and your motorhome rental company will ask you not to (see Chapter 3). But the bus drivers know how, and they do so with verve. The scenic, but bumpy, trip up to Cape Reinga was topped off by a rollicking run down Ninety Mile Beach (it's actually only 64 miles; the guy who measured it must have spun his wheels a bit). Seriously, the beach is sacred to the Maoris, who believe that the souls of their dead travel its misty path to Cape Reinga, where they depart through the roots of an ancient tree for their legendary homeland of "Hawaiki." The cape is also the meeting place of the Pacific Ocean and the Tasman Sea. It's a beautiful spot, marked by a picturesque lighthouse.

The Ninety Mile Beach Motor Camp is located 18 km north of Kaitaia, but we continued south, cutting off on a twisty, corrugated dirt road down to the ferry landing at Kohukohu. We spent a peaceful night there.

Tourist launches on Milford Sound. (Courtesy New Zealand Tourist and Publicity Office)

A lakeside rest area near Queenstown. (Photo by David Shore)

Day 6—Kohukohu to Helensville (266 km, 4 hrs.)

We took the ferry in the early morning mist across Hokianga Harbour to Rawene. It was a nice trip, during which we had an enlightening conversation with a Maori man about life in that part of the country. The harbour is ringed by small resorts and Maori settlements. (You can bypass the difficult dirt road—and the ferry—by continuing down S.H. 1 to Ohaeawai and turning right onto P.H. 12.) A small road took us from the ferry landing at Rawene up to P.H. 12, which we followed over to the western side of the island and down to the Waipaua Kauri Forest. It was a fascinating ride over a mostly dirt, but not too bad, forest road through dense ferns and towering trees. A short, well-signposted footpath took us into the bush to see Tane Mahuta (God of the Forest), the largest known Kauri tree in New Zealand. An impressive sight, it is 51.5 metres (167 feet) tall and 13.77 metres (45 feet) in girth, with an estimated age of 1,200 years.

New Zealand was once covered with Kauris, with trunks so tall, straight and smooth they were widely used as masts for sailing ships. The few stands that survived are now protected by government proclamation in this last great Kauri forest.

We drove 2 km down another dirt road to the forest headquarters, where they have displays of Kauri history and lore, Kauri gum, and stuffed examples of native birds. Across the road is a well-preserved gumdigger's shack dating from New Zealand's gum rush days.

We continued on down P.H. 12, rejoining S.H. 1 at Brynderwyn and turning onto P.H. 16 at Wellsford. This took us down to the thermal resort town of Helensville, where we found the Parakai Hot Springs pools and motor camp crowded and noisy. Right around the corner, however, was a quiet little motel called the Mineral Park. We had its indoor spa pool and swimming pool all to ourselves after we hooked up to one of the three power points.

Day 7—Helensville to Whitianga (271 km, 4¹/₂ hrs.)

Heading down S.H. 1, straight through Auckland on the motorway, we stopped at a large fruit stand in the Indian settlement of Bombay. There we were introduced to some delicious local fruits and exchanged stories in the parking lot with other travelers. Continuing on, we turned east on S.H. 2 and then northeast on P.H. 25 toward the Coromandel Peninsula. Thames is the big city there, once a roaring gold rush capital but now an industrial town. We followed the road north along the Firth of Thames, past swimming beaches and fishing spots. After passing the town of Coromandel the road turned east to cross the peninsula. It also turned to dirt, and got very rough and dusty. The scenery is spectacular in that wild, sparsely settled part of the world, but the road is among the worst in the country and definitely not suited to the large motorhome we were trying to drive on it. It was a slow, jarring 40 kilometres.

On the east coast, just above Whitianga, the pavement came back. We glided into town, seemingly floating on air, and stopped at the Whitianga Bay Motor Camp. It was just across the road from a beach on Mercury Bay, and we jumped right in. After a refreshing swim, we tried unsuccessfully to exhaust the camp shower's supply of hot water, then had a nice dinner as we watched the sunset light on the palisades across the bay.

Day 8—Whitianga to Rotorua (264 km, 3¹/₂ hrs.)

The motor camp owner was very helpful, letting us use her phone to make several calls to change our Cook Strait Ferry reservation. We just didn't want to leave the North Island as soon as we had planned. We finally got it changed, paid her for the long-distance charges, thanked her, and got on the road. We passed by Hot Water Beach, where on a cooler day we would be tempted to dig a hole in the sand and take a hot soak.

Continuing south on P.H. 25, we paused for lunch at

Waihi. What stopped us was a bakery advertising homemade hot steak pies, a favorite Kiwi street food. There were other interesting shops in this typically spic-and-span town, and we bought some fresh orange roughy for dinner after eating our steak pies in the motorhome, watching the townspeople walk by our windows.

Pushing ever southward, we soon came to Tauranga, on the Bay of Plenty. Originally a military town, it has grown into a major shipping port and agricultural center. There is a kiwifruit winery, and the National Citrus Festival is held here in August. Big-game fishing is reportedly very good around Mayor Island; the season runs from December to May. There are boats to take you view the active volcanoes on White Island, and Mount Maunganui stands above the best surfing beach on the east coast. We crossed the new toll-bridge there, and had to pay double because our motorhome was "heavy traffic" (over 3,000 kg). The toll collector actually apologized!

We then followed S.H. 2 past Te Puke, where a giant kiwifruit slice by the roadside tells you that you're in the "Kiwifruit Capital of the World." Tours of the orchards and kiwifruit everything can be had here. Turning right onto P.H. 33, we headed south to Rotorua. We expected a smarmy tourist trap, but we should have known better; this was New Zealand. Rotorua is full of tourist attractions and things to do, but the people were genuine, friendly, and helpful, and the prices were not inflated.

To do Rotorua right, we found that one must experience the three M's: Mineral baths, Maori culture and Mud pools. For the first, there are public baths like the opulent Polynesian Pools (east end of Hinemoa Street), or motor camps, notably Lakeside, Cosy Cottage, and Rotorua Thermal. The local tourist information office can direct you to these, as well as everything else in town. Hot water is not hard to find in Rotorua; it's the capital of the Volcanic Plateau, and there are steam vents all over town. Instead of backyard barbecues, homeowners here build steamers over holes they have bored in the ground. They also use the free steam to heat their homes and swimming pools. That's one reason why Rotorua is one of New Zealand's fastest-growing residential areas. An evening walk among the wafting plumes of steam gave us an eerie feeling. The Maoris were right: this is a mystical place.

We went first to the Lakeside Motor Camp, where they were cleaning the spa pools. No mineral baths here tonight, they said. So we chose the Cosy Cottage M.C., a few yards up the street. The hot pool was not spectacular, but it was pleasant. Rotorua Thermal M.C. is located adjacent to the Whakarewarewa Thermal Reserve, and has appropriate facilities.

For the second M, we attended a Maori "Hangi," a traditional feast followed by a ceremony of song and dance depicting the history of the Maoris' coming to New Zealand and the love story of Hinemoa and Tutanekai. Many of the tourist hotels offer slick versions of this, but we opted for the innocent and enthusiastic amateur presentation by Maori teenagers at St. Faith's Church. We also picked up some Maori culture at Whakarewarewa, the major thermal area, where we saw displays of Maori art and buildings.

Just outside the main entrance to "Whaka," as the locals call it, is the Maori Arts & Crafts Institute, a museum-like showroom full of large and small wood carvings, jewelry, and other items of art and handicrafts. Behind the showroom is the workshop and school where you can see the carvings being made. Adjoining the showroom is the gift shop, where you can spend a lot of money on sheepskins, sweaters, and $500 leather jackets as well as other tourist items.

The third M represents just one of the thermal wonders we found at Whakarewarewa. There were geysers, boiling blue pools, and hot springs, as well as mud pools that looked like bubbling cauldrons of thick soup. The rotten egg-like smell of sulfur, jokingly called "Soir de Rotorua," pervades the air, but we soon got used to it. Many people claim that they don't smell it at all after a while.

We slept well in the cool night air, and were awakened in the morning by a chorus of quacking. Campgrounds usually have feral dogs and cats looking for handouts, but here we had ducks. They made the rounds of all the motorhomes like traveling minstrels, offering entertainment for bits of bread.

After a morning soak in the spa pool, we were off to the Agrodome. It was a lot more fun than we expected from a sheep show, and no written description can do it justice: a stage full of champion rams representing all the different breeds raised in New Zealand, all described in terms of the quality of their wool, what kind of terrain and grass they like, and where in New Zealand they are raised. This is more entertaining than one might think. The host, a famous shearer, demonstrates how it's done, and then introduces the sheepdogs, who have a grand time doing tricks and running and jumping on the backs of the sheep.

After that you can have your picture taken with the rams and the dogs, and then milk a cow and pet a goat. Then the whole crowd is led outside to see a demonstration of sheepdog prowess, with a couple of dogs herding a small flock around a pen. Great fun to watch. Before or after the show, you can stroll through the native bush near the main building.

All of the native plants along the path are labeled, and it's cool and shady in there. But suddenly you find yourself looking not at a plant, but at a giant bird's leg. You look up, and up, and realize that you are confronting a ten-foot-tall moa (stuffed, of course, since the bird is extinct). Several moas are standing there, looking sort of goofy; a cross between Big Bird and Ollie the Dragon. They're just reconstructions based on a few bones and a lot of imagination, but they give a vague idea of what the moas must have looked like, tramping through the ferns 300 years ago.

The Agrodome is also a good place to shop for gifts and those hand-knit wool sweaters you've been promising yourself. The prices are as low as you'll find, and there are often some nice items in the sale bins. Shopping in general is best in Rotorua, where you'll find everything you need or want at reasonable prices.

Day 9—Rotorua to Taupo (82 km, 1¹/₂ hrs.)

Having seen everything we had time for, we reluctantly left Rotorua, heading south on S.H. 5. We passed several more thermal areas and hot springs, and rode alongside the Waikato River for a short time. Just before we reached the town of Wairakei, we crested a hill and glimpsed through the trees a sight we could hardly believe. We were shocked to see the unmistakable form of a nuclear cooling tower. It was identical to many we had seen in France and Germany and at Three Mile Island. How could this be, here in this aggressively anti-nuclear country that had given up valuable defense alliances and trade agreements in order to remain nuclear-free? That question still burned as we passed the spectacular Huka Falls, where the Waikato narrows and spews its waters over a 36-foot cliff.

The town of Taupo fronts along S.H. 5 as it skirts the edge of the vast lake. The trout fishing here is legendary, and the town has other attractions, but we had spent too much time in Rotorua and at various stops on the way down. It was time to look for a motor camp.

We found the one we were looking for: DeBrett's Thermal Motor Camp, right on the corner of Highways 1 and 5 after you turn towards Napier. It is one of the best places in New Zealand to park your rig, and probably the best we have experienced. Not only is it clean, well-run and less expensive than most, with nice landscaping and facilities, it's located on a hill with a fine view of Lake Taupo and the volcanoes on the far side. What's more, this place features its own Thermal Valley, a lovely little gorge over a hot spring which they have developed into a spa complex.

There are three large pools, hot, warm, and cold, and private spa pool rooms, all drained and cleaned nightly.

There's not even a sulfur smell. The cost? One dollar extra (for guests only), and another if you want a private room. We preferred the public pools; they're outdoors and the evening was perfect, and there were only a few other people there.

The proprietors were friendly and helpful. By the way, they answered our burning question by mentioning the new cooling towers at the Wairakei *geothermal* power station, which make it easier on the environment by cooling the steamy water before releasing it into the Waikato. New Zealand is still nuclear free.

Day 10—Taupo to Waipawa (217 km, 3 hrs.)

In the morning we were back on S.H. 5, heading southeast toward Napier. We had heard and read about this unique city, rebuilt in 1931 in Art Deco style after being destroyed by an earthquake, so we were curious to see it. But it was a long and scenic ride to get there.

We passed through the Kaingaroa State Forest, a huge stand of "exotic" pine trees. Farther down the road we passed a rest area whose sign was so obscure that we missed it and had to turn around and go back to it. It was worth the trouble, though; the rest area was on top of a hill overlooking Waipunga Falls. It was a pleasant surprise, but how many travelers have missed it? We met a young Kiwi couple traveling on motorcycles, and had an informative conversation about unemployment and the effect of "the dole," or welfare system, on young people's desire to work. "There are plenty of jobs to be had," our new friends assured us as we all gazed at the hidden falls. Don't miss them; the rest area is on the left side of the road, about 20 km south of Rangitaiki. Maybe they'll put up a bigger sign by the time you get there.

After a bit of mountain driving and superb vistas of the surrounding forest lands, we descended to the east coast and turned south on S.H. 2, which took us into Napier. (Time restrictions made us forego the East Cape on this first trip, with its magnificent beaches, hot springs and scenic walks.)

Bearing left at the fork, we stuck hard by the seashore as the road undulated around the base of high, sheer palisades. We soon found ourselves on the Marine Parade, the shoreline drive of this unique city. It was April, autumn was in the air, and we sensed the slightly sad, seedy atmosphere of a British seaside resort. The place seemed deserted. There was a nocturnal Kiwi house, though, where we saw some interesting native birds and introduced animals, all displayed in their preferred low-light situation. The Kiwis were quite entertaining to watch.

Leaving our motorhome parked on the Marine Parade, we crossed the street and cut through a video game arcade (at the suggestion of the local tourist office) and emerged in the heart of the famed Art Deco downtown area. The architecture was interesting, in a minor sort of way, and most of it was well-restored.

Back on the road, we rolled through some pleasant countryside, passing the wineries of Hawke's Bay and the turnoff to the Gannet Sanctuary at Cape Kidnappers before coming to Hastings, where we were a few days late for the Highland Games. They're held during the Easter weekend, and Patty's Scottish soul was yearning to see them. But we had stayed in the warm, soft embrace of the Northland too long; there's just too much to experience in this country!

Below Hastings we stopped at a roadside fruit stand that had in its front yard a tree bearing apples of over 200 different kinds from branches that had been grafted on. We bought a selection of fruits and drove away, happily chomping on Nashi (often called Japanese pears, actually half pear, half apple). Continuing down to Waipawa, we followed a little yellow fingerboard to the Waipawa Motor Camp, to the left of S.H. 2, down a small street. It was very simple—just a field with power points sticking up out of the grass, but very clean and neat. It was run by a nice old man who kept a lending library of once-popular books donated by and for the guests. We added one, too.

Day 11—Waipawa to Picton (285 km + ferry, 8 hrs.)

Dannevirke is a charming town about 60 km south of Waipawa. Originally a Danish settlement, its name means "Danes' work." We saw a doctor here after Patty had an asthma attack as we passed through the area north of town. He prescribed some medicine, and the prescription was filled at the chemist's. We also changed money at the bank and bought beer at the bottle store. Everyone was friendly and welcoming to us. A nice experience.

At Woodville we stopped for a map conference. There were two ways to get to Wellington: Highways 3, 87, and 1, or straight down S.H. 2. A policeman saw us looking at the map and offered to help. He described the scenery and road conditions of both alternatives, trying to be as helpful as possible. We chose S.H. 2 and were on our way.

At Greytown we found our Devonshire Tea. It was at an old English tearoom called Turkey Red. The perfect thing at the perfect time (we were tired and hungry) and the perfect place: Greytown lived up to its name that day. We cruised on into Wellington feeling well-fed and happy. We headed for the ferry terminal first, since we had easy directions from S.H. 2, which had, become a multi-lane motorway. When we arrived at the ferry ticket booth, we found a hand-lettered sign in the window that read simply, "PLEASE WAIT HERE." So we waited.

We waited some more, and at last; the harbormaster arrived. Although we were scheduled to sail on the 8:00 A.M. ferry the next day, he said he could get us on the next one, leaving at 6:00 P.M. We had an appointment in Christchurch the next afternoon, and this would give us more time to enjoy the South Island on the way down. (We had arranged to trade our six-berth motorhome, which we had realized was bigger than we needed or wanted, for a two-berth van.) The harbormaster told us to park and wait some more.

We waited, and soon we saw the ferry come in. It was a huge, pea-green ship with doors in the rear. It backed in and started disgorging trains. Yes, trains. The ferry service is run by the New Zealand Railways, who developed it primarily to connect its rail lines between the North and South Islands. So the trains roll off and on first, then the motorhomes are fitted in between them (it's a strange feeling when you're sitting in your rig on arrival and the trains start moving all around you). The cars go on a different deck, and they miss all the fun. Up on the passenger decks there are lots of different places to sit. You can choose a seat on the "sun deck" up on top, stroll around the other open decks, go inside and sit in one of the lounges, some of which have TVs, or spend some time in the semi-tacky bar cafeteria, where the food is edible if not gourmet. You're free to move around, and there's plenty of time to try them all on the 3½-hour cruise. There is a first class lounge if you have the appropriate ticket, but it's usually quite full of tobacco smoke. Our favorite place is the second class lounge, where you can sit in commodious booths with tables and big leather cushions. If it's not too crowded you can lie down and nap away the hours. You cannot stay in your motorhome during the voyage.

It was 10:00 P.M. when we landed in Picton, and in the dark we missed Alexanders Motor Park, around a few corners from the ferry landing on Canterbury Street. Instead we headed on down S.H. 1 toward Blenheim. A few km down the road we came upon a deer sanctuary which looked like a dandy freecamping spot until we saw the sign prohibiting it. The proprietor of the motel next door said he didn't normally take motorhomes and had no power points or other facilities, but we were welcome to park behind the motel at no charge. We had a nice conversation about the area, and he pointed out the Southern Cross in the clear night sky. Later we drifted off to sleep to the tune of the stags bellowing in the deer sanctuary.

Day 12—Picton to Christchurch (350 km, 7 hrs.)

The road (S.H. 1) down to Christchurch passes through Blenheim, statistically New Zealand's sunniest city and center of the Marlborough wine-growing area. Wineries line the roadside, but we opted to avoid the temptation of wine-tasting while driving. Besides, we had this appointment. Running right along the coast for about 120 km, we saw some beautiful black-sand beaches and rock formations. The road turned inland at Oaro, and soon we began seeing hand-lettered signs heralding "COOKED CRAYS." We stopped and Patty picked out what turned out to be a very tasty lobster.

We pressed on into Christchurch and promptly got lost. But people were helpful with directions and we found the Budget depot just before closing time. We had caused them a good bit of trouble by asking to switch our Auckland-based motorhome for a Christchurch-based van, and our timing was not the best, but they were very nice about it and even helped us move in. (It was amazing how quickly we had expanded into the space of that large motorhome, and how small the van seemed, even though we normally travel by van. We quickly got used to it again, though, and were much happier driving the smaller vehicle.) They gave us directions to a good motor camp nearby and we were on our way.

The Amber Park Motor Camp was nice enough, and had a free telephone for use by the guests. Its main attraction was that it was on S.H. 1 as it headed south out of town.

Day 13—Christchurch to Fairlie (217 km, 3 hrs.)

After a brief walk around Cathedral Square we hit the road to our next adventure: a farm stay. We were to be the guests of Leighton and Shirley Jones on their sheep ranch in the high country of Canterbury. The area looks a lot like Montana, with rolling green hills, sharp, picturesque mountains, and crystal-clear air, not to mention sheep everywhere. It can get quite cool up there in the fall, as we were to find out that evening. Central heating in a New Zealand farmhouse means one fireplace in the living room. The Joneses had mercifully provided electric blankets in the guest bedroom.

They were wonderful hosts. We talked about farm life in New Zealand, ate some hearty home-cooked meals, and enjoyed their teenage son's account of the day's Rugby game. Shirley pulled out her spinning wheel and showed us how she takes wool from her own sheep and turns it into beautiful hand-knit sweaters and other garments, some for sale to tourist shops. A friend from a neighboring farm dropped in and we all sat around the fire drinking Steinlager and kiwifruit liqueur and talking late into the night. We slept well that night.

Next morning we rode around in Leighton's Japanese jeep and watched the dogs working enthusiastically with the sheep. He proudly showed us his own jet boat, powered by a big American V8 engine. The whole visit gave us a unique insider's perspective on everyday life in New Zealand, the best kind of travel experience.

Day 14—Fairlie to Mount Cook (148 km, 3 hrs.)

Reluctantly leaving the farm, we took S.H. 8 out of Fairlie, bound for Mount Cook. When we passed Lake Tekapo and the Tekapo River, where Leighton had said he likes, to run his jet boat, the scenery began to get better. Golden poplars shimmered along the roadsides, rivers sparkled as they rushed over rapids in the bright sunshine, and the glacial lakes glowed a beautiful turquoise, reflecting the snow-capped peaks of the Southern Alps. We stopped at a fruit "stall" or stand, where the people were as sunny as the skies. They informed us that this was normal weather for early autumn. Soon we came to P.H. 80 and turned right, toward

Mount Cook. The road took us along the edge of Lake Pukaki, whose aquamarine color comes from its origins in the pure ice of the Tasman Glacier.

As we rounded a curve, the majestic peak of Mount Cook swung into view. It was an awe-inspiring sight, sharp and glistening with snow against the deep blue sky. At 12,349 feet, it's the tallest mountain in Australasia. We wanted to take a ski plane ride and see it up close, but a heavy cloud cover came in and flights were stopped for the day (it was late afternoon). After driving around Mount Cook Village and the luxurious Hermitage hotel, we drove back down the road to Glentanner Park Motor Camp. We were in high country and there was definitely an autumn nip in the air. The camp store had a nice selection of handknit sweaters and we decided it was time to succumb. Post-season prices helped finalize that decision, and soon we were warm and elegant, Kiwi style.

Day 15—Mount Cook to Cromwell (202 km, 3 hrs.)

There was frost on the grass when we awoke, but soon the sun broke through the mist and shone brightly on the snow-capped mountains. We went back to Mount Cook airport and climbed aboard a ski plane. The flight was spectacular; the air was so clear that the mountains looked much closer than they actually were, adding to the excitement. We landed on the Tasman Glacier with a planeload of Japanese tourists, who had a snowball fight. It was fascinating to dig through the three-inch snow cover to the solid blue ice of the glacier.

Having seen much more of his mountain than Captain Cook ever did, we pointed our perky little van southward again, stopping for lunch and fuel at the unearthly village of Twizel. Built in the 1960s to house construction workers on the nearby power station, its sterile, uniform buildings and nearly deserted shopping center give it the atmosphere of an abandoned moon colony. We moved on to Omarama, a more human town.

Further on down the road we crossed the Lindis Pass and descended into the old gold rush country, finally coming into Cromwell. We did some shopping in this interesting town, and followed a local's directions to the Sunhaven Motor Camp. It was located at the end of a street whose name, according to the street sign, was NEPLUSULTRA. People pronounced it in various oblivious ways.

It was in Cromwell that we gave up trying to find the filler inlet to the fresh water tank on our newly-acquired Toyota campervan. Rather embarrassed, we called the Budget office in Christchurch. They didn't laugh at us but informed us that it was cleverly hidden behind the jack in the step-down well inside the sliding side door. Of course, we said; how could we have missed that?

Day 16—Cromwell to Te Anau (256 km, 3¹/₂ hours)

Just outside Cromwell we joined S.H. 6, which took us past the Roaring Meg power station in the Kawarau Gorge. There's a nice creekside picnic area across the road. This is gold rush country, and the Kawarau Gorge Mining Centre offers a look at some of the old mining equipment and an interesting bridge walk across the gorge. A bit farther on was the turnoff to Arrowtown, an old gold rush town reminiscent of those in California. The main street is now lined with tourist shops.

Between the town and S.H. 6, though, is Lake Hayes, so smooth and tranquil it mirrors the surrounding mountains. We had lunch at one of the picnic tables set up on the shore. (They are reached by a small dirt driveway leading down from the road to a gate. Open it and pass through; it's public property.)

From there it was on into Queenstown, a beautiful city nestled in the mountains on the shore of Lake Wakatipu. There was so much to do and see there, we decided to go on to Te Anau and catch it on the way back when we would have more time.

We followed the shore of the lake south on S.H. 6, passing breathtaking scenery and stopping often to take pictures. At a lovely tree-shaded rest area with a pebble beach right on the lake, we stuck our toes in the clear water. It was cold. The road continued past Kingston, home of an antique train called the *Kingston Flyer*. Tickets are available for its short run through the surrounding countryside.

At Five Rivers we took a right turn for a shortcut down to Mossburn, where another right put us on P.H. 94. We followed that road into Te Anau. The best motor camp there, we were to find out later, is the first one you see when you turn left into the town. The Te Anau Motor Park is in a wooded hillside setting, offering lake views from most sites. The Mountain View Caravan Park, just past the town center, is also very good.

Day 17—Te Anau to Milford Sound & Back (242 km, 9 hrs.)

Te Anau is best known as the jumping-off place for the Milford Track and the Milford Road. The Track, a strenuous five-day hike, is booked up months in advance. We chose the road, and we chose not to drive it. The Fiordland Coach/Boat tour was worth the NZ$50 each (NZ$65 in high season). Not only could we both look at the scenery instead of the road, but the tour guide's lively commentary let us know what we were looking at. The bus was quite comfortable, and it stopped periodically for short walks and points of interest. A short side trip down the Lower Hollyford Road took us to Murray Gunn's Motor Camp, a rustic place with a museum and store. It's the starting place for the Hollyford Track.

The bus was a good place to meet other travelers and share experiences and tips. It took us right to the boat landing on Milford Sound, where we were ushered aboard a large sightseeing boat (the smaller ones are better; they can get closer to the seals basking on the rocks, and sometimes nose right into the waterfalls). The box lunch served on board, paid for in advance with the tour ticket, was not memorable. It's better to save your NZ$6 and bring along the food of your choice in your day pack. Free coffee and tea are served on the boat. It was a spectacular trip, bus and boat. It took all day, from 8:00 A.M. to 5:00 P.M. The bus picked us up at our motor camp and returned us there. The tour can be booked at the office of either motor camp or at the Fiordland office in town.

A similar tour on the same route is run by the Magic Bus, geared to (but not restricted to) a younger clientele. The price is a few dollars cheaper, and a 15 percent discount is offered to motorhomers staying at Te Anau Motor Park. Children under 15 ride free. The bus is less luxurious than the Fiordland coach, but the tour is choreographed with the appropriate music for the scenery, and ice cream and coffee are served. It's not associated with the Magic Bus in Europe.

The Te Anau Motor Park does not require you to book a two-night stay if you take the Milford tour (as does Mountain View). You can leave your rig in their safe parking area after one night, then move on after the tour if you wish.

DRIVING YOURSELF

Because of the hazards and inconveniences involved, we do not recommend driving the Milford Road in your van or motorhome, and neither does the rental company who is trusting you with it, if you're renting (see Chapter 3). The rough, narrow dirt road demands constant attention, and the scenery is too good to miss. What's more, the tour buses take up most of the roadway, and getting out of their way can be tricky. If you insist on doing it yourself, drive to the Sound in the morning and back in the afternoon to be going the same way they are.

Once you've arrived at the Sound you can park free in the lot across from the Milford Hotel and use the public toilet block there, or go back half a mile to the Milford Lodge, where there are hookups and showers for a small fee. But fuel will cost you as much as one bus ticket, and you still must pay for the boat ride. In high season the pre-booked passengers will have priority, and you may have to wait.

Day 18—*Te Anau to Queenstown (154 km, 2 hrs.)*

Te Anau is a nice town, very scenic and interesting, and we wanted to explore it a bit more before we left. On the road to Manapouri, just south of the Te Anau Motor Park, is the Te Anau Wildlife Center Birdlife Reserve. On a tip from a local, we investigated and found three of the very rare flightless birds known as the Takahe (see Chapter 9). We had a good time sticking blades of grass through the fence, which they ate enthusiastically from our hands, even though they were knee-deep in the stuff.

Continuing down the same road, we followed the signs to the Kepler Track, a hiking trail through a fern and beech forest sparkling with little creeks and studded with odd mushrooms. An easy, level half-hour walk, the track took us to a lovely secluded beach with a picnic table and barbecue. It goes on in several different directions. The track begins across the dam from the car park, which is a good freecamping place.

Tearing ourselves away from Te Anau, we retraced our route back to Queenstown. Nowhere else have we seen a place more ideally suited to so many different forms of recreation, nor have we seen more forms of recreation in one place. After looking around the town and shopping for dinner, we checked in at the Queenstown Motor Park, a large, well-designed camp situated above the town and overlooking the lake.

We took a walk around the grounds after dark, and noticed a large, brightly-lit object floating in the night sky. It seemed to be hovering right above us, and we were puzzled. When we saw a light descending slowly from it, we really started wondering. Then we realized that the motor camp was at the base of a nearly-vertical cliff, and our UFO was the restaurant at the top of the gondola lift. It was almost a quarter of a mile above us, planted on terra firma.

Day 19—Queenstown to Wanaka (117 km, 1³/₄ hrs.)

Queenstown put on her best weather for us this day, and it was a joy to be outdoors here. We rode that gondola up to the restaurant and drank free tea as we drank in the gorgeous views of the town, the lake and the mountains all around. There's a gift shop and a movie theatre up there, too, and helicopters drop off flightseers on the helipad. You can hike to the top as well, and we noticed that since they don't check gondola tickets for the trip down, some hikers were descending in style for free. Near the base of the gondolas is the Autoshow, a classic car museum with an interesting collection which includes the world's first ski plane (hanging from the ceiling) and a motorhome from 1926, complete with a pot-bellied stove, porcelain pedestal sink and red velvet sofa bed. It had toured the U.S. in its day.

Before we left Queenstown we visited a brand-new upscale motor camp called Creeksyde. This deluxe facility features a unique circular building surrounded by large pie-shaped sites. In the building are luxury baths, a carpeted lounge, a large kitchen with picture windows so that mothers can watch their children, and upstairs meeting rooms and bedrooms for rent. There are even hookups for telephone and cable TV.

We drove on to Wanaka, a scenic drive through almost totally unpopulated mountains. Just past the Arrowtown turnoff we took a left and started up P.H. 89, which we thought would be a nice shortcut. After we climbed slowly up the tight switchback road, the pavement ended and it got very rough. A motorhome driver coming the other way signaled emphatically that it was not a suitable road. We believed him and went back to S.H. 6, the long but smooth way to Wanaka.

There are several motor camps near Wanaka. We chose Penrith Park, a rustic but adequate camp on the lake shore. The sunset across the lake was beautiful.

Day 20—Wanaka to Fox Glacier (267 km, 5 hrs.)

This is a very scenic and interesting, albeit slow, drive over the Haast Pass through the Southern Alps to the west coast. Leaving Lake Wanaka, S.H. 6 runs along the edge of gorgeous Lake Hawea, its deep (1,345 ft.) waters shining a deep blue. We passed a little beach nestled in The Neck, a narrow point of the lake. There was a motorhome free-camped there, its owners probably fishing.

After that the road began a steep, winding climb toward the Haast Pass, degenerating to dirt for stretches and some-times pinching down to one lane for road works or slips. It's slow going, but the scenery gets better and better as it threads its way through the misty green mountains, passing such worthwhile stops as the Blue Pools, Fantail Falls, and Thunder Creek Falls. Soon we descended to the wet, jungly coast, following the Haast River from the Gates of Haast bridge.

State Highway 6 turned north at the coast and continued up to the town of Fox Glacier, which has a general store, a food market, and a restaurant. We met a nice Aussie couple enjoying a trip given to them by their children after years of building a business. Their aging Suntrek motorhome, which came with a package tour, was causing them a few annoying problems, but even that failed to dull their enthusiasm. The weather that day was not the best for flying, but they took a NZ$100 helicopter ride over the glacier anyway. "You only live once," they said.

We took the small road through the forest to the glacier. Along the road were signs showing where the receding glacier face had been in years past. The road led to a parking lot, from which we walked a track to the glacier face itself.

It's an experience not to be missed. The huge mass of ice

looms up grayly, choking the gouged-out chasm with cave-riddled ice, dropping chunks with a boom like a cannon. A sign warns you to keep a safe distance, but hired guides will take you right up to walk on the glacier, providing proper footgear and the knowhow to keep you out of trouble.

There's a small motor camp down a road that runs west from the highway. It's adequate but far from luxurious. We didn't care; it, was raining and we stayed in our cozy van. We slept well with the sound of the rain on the roof.

Day 21—Fox Glacier to Westport (307 km, 4 hrs.)

When we awoke it was still overcast, but the rain had stopped. We headed north to the Franz Josef Glacier and found it quite a different experience from Fox. The trek from the car park to the glacier was longer, nearly an hour over interesting terrain. But when you first see the glacier, shining white with blue highlights, you'll be glad you did it. If you must choose between the two glaciers, this is the more spectacular. There were Keas flying and swaggering around the car park, clowning for handouts (we never have seen them eating windshield wipers, despite all the warnings). We continued on up the coast, past the greenstone exhibits and glass-blowing factory at Hokitika, and the Motukiekie Rocks. The Pancake Rock formations and blowholes at Punakaiki National Park were fascinating and definitely worth a stop.

Westport, 6 km up P.H. 67, has pretty beaches, a bustling main street and a very good motor camp called Howard Holiday Park.

Day 22—Westport to Nelson (230 km, 4 hrs.)

This day's trip took us through the very scenic Buller Gorge. Highway 6 turned inland from Westport to snake along the Buller River, broad, still, and green in the deep shadowy cleft. The road is sealed all the way and quite pleasant to drive, even though it gets quite twisty and steep at times and even has some single-lane stretches. It's a popular truck route, but the big eighteen-wheelers (mostly American brands, like Mack and Kenworth) are herded along by courteous drivers. They'll pull over and let you pass on long, slow upgrades (a sign on the back of one trailer read: "GOT THE STRENGTH; HAVE YOU THE TIME?") It's wise to pull over and get out of *their* way as they career down the other side.

A nice place to stop for lunch is the Lyell Creek Rest Area, 72 km out of Westport. It's a lovely mountain meadow, with picnic tables, toilets, water, and interesting walkways to gold mining relics and the site of a former town nearby. The area is maintained by the Department of Lands and Survey, and there's an honesty box in which you should drop a dollar if you spend the night. The one drawback here is the sandflies. Bring insect repellent.

Near Murchison we passed the Riverview Motor Camp, a grassy lawn by the river shaded by big trees. But it was too early to stop, and we pressed on to Nelson. As we entered the city a large roadside sign listed all the motor camps in town. We followed the signs to the Maitai Motor Camp, a city-owned camp in a peaceful valley, next to the golf course

The setting was nice and the facilities adequate. There is a footpath along the river for a bucolic sunset walk.

Day 23—Nelson to Wellington (105 km + ferry, 5 ½ hrs.)

We took a quick look around Nelson, a lovely port city with what is called the most equable climate in New Zealand. It's curled around a wide, shallow bay and has parks and flowers and tree-filled valleys.

Leaving the north side of town on S.H. 6, we climbed mighty pine-forested mountain Slopes with perfect picnic and freecamping spots with water and toilets. These are just 15 km north of Nelson. There's also a nice sylvan motor camp at the Pelorus River bridge. The road follows the Pelorus up to Havelock, where the Marlborough Sounds begin.

The Pelorus mail launch cruise leaves here at 9:30 A.M. for a trip to the remote settlements in this maze of fiords. Tickets are NZ$35 each.

From here S.H. 6 makes a wide loop through Blenheim and on up to Picton, but we opted for the scenic route. The Queen Charlotte Drive winds along the shoreline for most of its 37 km, rising high above the Sound and dipping down into cozy little inlets with fine beaches and a few houses. At Momorangi Bay there's a nice motor camp with a gas station and a small store. The motor camp has boats for hire ranging from small canoes to cabin cruisers. We had a Jaffa milk shake (chocolate and orange), and continued on to Picton and the ferry landing.

It was a beautiful day for a boat trip through the Marlborough Sounds, and we enjoyed the ferry ride in the clear sunshine. The ferry is a good place to meet other travelers and compare notes. When we arrived in Wellington it was late, so we headed straight for the city-run Hutt Park Motor Camp, the only one in town (the next one is 45 minutes north). It's not on the main road and it's hard to find, so here are some directions to help you:

As you drive off the ferry, follow the signs reading "NORTH" onto S.H. 2. Take the Hutt Valley turnoff to your right and exit at PETONE. Go 4 km along the Esplanada to the roundabout and follow the "MOTOR CAMP" signs.

Hutt Park is a clean, modern camp with reasonable rates.

Day 24—Wellington to Paraparaumu (54 km, 1 hr.)

Wellington is a sophisticated city with interesting architecture and an atmosphere like the Mayfair district of London without the snobbery. It's a shopper's paradise, with arcades and restaurants galore. We visited the Parliament building and the unique round adminstrative building known as the "Beehive." At 2:00 P.M. we saw the opening of Parliament (arrive at the tour desk at 1:50, Tuesday and Thursday only).

Beehive tours leave every half-hour on weekdays between 9:30 A.M. and 4:00 P.M. The Alexander Turnbull National Library, just up Molesworth Street from Parliament, houses exhibits of New Zealand art as well as books. The gift shop has a large selection of posters, postcards and quality New Zealand gift items.

Leaving Wellington on S.H. 1, we passed through some pleasant towns before coming to the new Lindale Motor Home & Caravan Park, just north of Paraparaumu. This deluxe camp has an award-winning layout, with small hills affording some privacy between sites. It is adjacent to the Lindale Farm Park,

Day 25—Paraparaumu to Turangi (276 km, 4 hrs.)

The Southward Car Museum is one of the best we've seen. A short way up the road from Lindale, it houses the personal collection of industrialist Len Southward, who has placed it in a trust administered by the government. Among the "stars" of the exhibit are Marlene Dietrich's Cadillac, gangster Mickey Cohen's bullet-proof limousine, and an 1895 Benz. With over 200 cars, it's the largest collection in the Southern Hemisphere. We met Southward himself, a cheerful man who obviously loves his cars. "Ten cents she'll go first pop," he challenged, walking over to the Benz, then turned the crank and started the oldest car in New Zealand.

Continuing on up S.H. 1, we stopped in Levin to cash a traveler's check and shop for dinner. It's a clean, bustling town. From there the road runs through fruit and vegetable country. There are many roadside stands with interesting produce (fine strawberries and raspberries in summer) and low prices. Above Waiouru the land turns to desert, with rolling terrain covered in tussock and strange naturally-carved cliffs.

It was nearly dark when we reached Turangi, on the edge of Tongariro National Park. We were looking for the

Turangi Holiday Park, but there were no fingerboards or other signs to help us. We asked directions in a petrol station and found it. Originally built to house hydroelectric workers, it looks like an army camp, but has bathtubs. It's better to go 3 km farther west on P.H. 41 to Tokaanu Thermal Pools, have a hot soak and freecamp in the parking lot.

Day 26—Turangi to Wanganui (197 km, 3 hrs.)

We discovered Tokaanu in the morning light. In addition to public and private thermal pools and a sauna, there is a thermal reserve with a walking path that takes you around and among steaming ponds, bubbling mud pools, and various other examples of thermal activity. Six km west on P.H. 41 at Waihi is a rest area located high on a mountainside with magnificent views of Lake Taupo and the surrounding volcanoes and countryside. A worthwhile side trip.

We went back through Tokaanu and turned south on P.H. 47A toward the Chateau Tongariro, a famous national park hotel. Along the road there is a sign announcing the Rotopounamu Lake Track, an idyllic 20-minute walk to a secret lake high in a volcanic crater with sandy beaches and a track all the way around it (1½ hrs. more). Continuing south, the road rejoins P.H. 47. We turned east on P.H. 48 to the Chateau.

The Whakapapa Motor Camp across the road resembles an American national park campground, with sites separated by trees and bush. The Tongariro National Park Visitor Center has a fascinating audiovisual presentation about the volcanic activity all around you.

Back down P.H. 48, we took a left on P.H. 47 and another onto S.H. 4 toward Wanganui. This is hilly, grassy farm country with isolated clumps of huge trees and ubiquitous sheep. South of Parapara there's a rest area with a stairway down to a spectacular view of Raukawa Falls. It's worth a stop.

Just north of Wanganui is a large, lovely rest area in a rural setting with lush grass and poplars by the river. We spent a peaceful night there after trying in vain to find the motor camp in town. Wanganui is a pleasant seaside city in a picturesque river valley.

Day 27—Wanganui to Stratford (142 km, 2 hrs.)

Turning west on S.H. 3, we drove through rolling farmland, out of sight of the coast. We were heading for another farm stay in the shadow of mighty Mt. Taranaki (also called Mt. Egmont) outside Stratford. Our best chance to see the South Taranaki coast was to be at Patea. It's a pleasant seaside resort town at the mouth of the Patea River, which flows through Stratford (once called Stratford-on-Patea) from its source in the snow-cap of Mt. Taranaki before meandering its way down to the sea. We turned left on Egmont Street. This took us down to Carlyle Beach Camp and a long curve of black sand beach backed by glittering dunes. The Patea Board Riders Club has its artfully-painted headquarters there, right next to a sign that reads "NO SURFING."

We passed through Hawera, and instead of turning north with S.H. 3, we continued west to Manaia for a back-roads approach to Mt. Taranaki. We came upon a road sign that read "CAUTION: CELEBRATION AHEAD." The Kapuni School was having its 100th birthday party, mostly in the road. They didn't expect much traffic. Another 15 km took us to the entrance of Egmont National Park, where we began an idyllic drive up the densely forested mountainside to Dawson Falls Lodge. We tramped one of several scenic tracks looping out from the Lodge.

Leaving the park, we followed the fingerboards to Stratford and on to the impressive dairy farm of Malcolm and Margaret Johnson. They were wonderful hosts, and we enjoyed their beautiful new house on a hill overlooking vast hilly paddocks (fields) of thick, bright-green grass being munched by contented cows and bulls. After an evening of lively conversation and a cold night's sleep (Kiwi central heating again), Malcolm took us on a tour of the farm and showed us his state-of-the-art milking operation. It was a very enjoyable visit, and we left with a jugful of fresh-squeezed milk.

Day 28—Stratford to Waitomo (217 km, 3 hrs.)

We followed S.H. 3 to New Plymouth, a pretty town and capital of the Taranaki area, and on up the coast through spectacular dark forested gorges and jagged seacoast with a wealth of grassy beaches and other freecamping spots. The turnoff to Waitomo is 11 km past Te Kuiti, a historic Maori town that is now heavily industrialized and not very inviting. On the road to Waitomo we stopped at Merrowvale, a restaurant with a model village laid out over a half acre, complete with a cigarette billboard and a working miniature railroad. Kids love it. They serve a wonderful Devonshire Tea, and although the tour buses stop there, the quality is high, the prices are low, and the people are genuinely nice.

The glowworm caves at Waitomo are not to be missed, even if you're used to fireflies. It's a wondrous experience, gliding silently in a boat beneath millions of starry lights that make intricate patterns on the dark cave ceilings. No talking is allowed. Tours run every half-hour from 9:30 A.M. to 4:30 P.M. Try to catch an early tour to avoid the busloads of boisterous tourists. You can do that by staying overnight at the motor camp across the road from the general store.

Day 29—Waitomo to South Auckland (254 km, 4 hrs.)

Back on S.H. 3, we drove up to Hamilton and turned west on P.H. 23. We wanted to see Raglan Harbour, legendary among surfers for its long break, and among others for its beauty. Raglan is a cute beach town, the beach is wide and pleasant, and the water was warm enough for swimming in late April.

We drove back through Hamilton and got on S.H. 1 toward Auckland, soon to find ourselves in one of New Zealand's few annual traffic jams. It was Anzac Day, the end of a four-day holiday weekend, and all the Aucklanders were headed home. We left the slow, bumper-to-bumper procession at Ramarama and headed for the South Auckland Motor Camp. It was adequate. We gazed up at the clear night sky and got our last look at the Southern Cross. We were to leave New Zealand the next day.

Day 30—South Auckland to Mangere (20 km, 1 hr.)

Mangere is the Auckland suburb near the International Airport, and most of the major motorhome rental companies have their depots there. The Budget depot was our ultimate destination, and after a last lunch of fish and chips in the park, we headed there.

But we had some trouble finding the place, because on that first day when we picked up our motorhome we hadn't noticed the names of the streets and roads leading to and from it. Some notes at that time would have helped. After bumbling around for a while, we found it, pulled in, and parked our little home on wheels for the last time.

The Budget folks welcomed us like old friends, asked about our experience and were genuinely concerned with any problems we might have had with the vehicles. They then drove us to the airport in time for our flight home.

On the plane we reminisced about the unique and wonderful experiences we had enjoyed on our first visit to this beautiful land. One thing was for sure: it was not to be our last.

Roadside ferns on the North Island. (Photo by David Shore)

Information Sources and Suggested Reading

New Zealand Tourist and Publicity Department Travel Offices

Suite 970, Alcoa Bldg.
One Maritime Plaza
San Francisco, CA 94111
Tel. (415) 788 7404

Suite 1530, Tishman Bldg.
10960 Wilshire Blvd.
Los Angeles, CA 90024
Tel. (213) 477 8241

630 Fifth Ave., Suite 530
New York, NY 10111
Tel. (212) 586 0060

Suite 1260, IBM Tower
701 West Georgia St.
Vancouver, B.C. V7Y 1B6
(604) 684 2117

Pamphlets and booklets available free from the New Zealand Tourist and Publicity Department Travel offices:

"Camp, Cabin & Caravan Accomodation." Camp & Cabin Assoc., 1987,

"Introducing New Zealand." NZTP (map)

"Motoring In New Zealand." The New Zealand Automobile Assoc., 1985

"The New Zealand Book." NZTP, 1987.

"New Zealand Festivals & Calendar of Events." NZTP, 1988.

"New Zealand Food." New Zealand Ministry of Foreign Affairs.

"The New Zealand Motoring Book." NZTP, 1987.

"New Zealand Museums, Historic Buildings, and Galleries." NZTP, 1983.

"New Zealand Outdoor Action Holidays." NZTP, 1987.

"Taste New Zealand in 1988." NZTP, 1987.

"Tread the Wine Trail." Hawke's Bay Vintners.

Books

Berlitz Travel Guide New Zealand. New York: Berlitz Publications, 1984. 128 pp. Compact little volume, but skimpy.

Bone, Robert W., edited by Susan Buckland. *The Maverick Guide to New Zealand.* 7th edition. Gretna, LA: Pelican Publishing Company, 1989. 350 pp. Practical and useful, written from an American point of view; revised by native New Zealander.

Burton, R. and M. Atkinson. *A Tramper's Guide to New Zealand's National Parks.* Edison, NJ: Hunter Publishing, 1988.

DuFresne, Jim. *Tramping in New Zealand.* Oakland, CA: Lonely Planet, 1982 (U.S. distributor—Bookpeople). 168 pp. Two definitive hiking guides.

Guy, Michael. *Michael Guy's Eating Out: The Guide to New Zealand Restaurants.* Sixth edition. Lyndon Publishing, 1987. 160 pp. Amusing short reviews of 400 restaurants, both good and bad.

Hannam, Gary and McIntosh, Leslie, editors. *Travellers New Zealand.* Auckland, NZ: Pacific Tourism Promotions, 1985. 264 pp. Tourist-oriented but much information, including addresses, local and phone numbers of excursion operators. Some maps, color photos.

King, Jane. *New Zealand Handbook.* Chico, CA: Moon Publications, 1987. 512 pp.

Leland, Louis S. Jr,. *A Personal Kiwi-Yankee Dictionary.* Gretna, LA: Pelican Publishing Company, 1984. 120 pp. Hilarious but extremely enlightening.

McDermott, John and Bobbye. *How to Get Lost and Found in Upgraded New Zealand.* Orafa Publications, 1988. Anecdotal and amusing, but very idiosyncratic and sexist.

McLauchlan, Gordon, ed. *New Zealand.* (Insight Guides) APA Productions, no date. (U.S. edition-Prentice-Hall) 339 pp. Many small color photos and drawings; is especially good for history.

Pope, Diana and Jeremy. *The Mobil Illustrated Guide to New Zealand.* Reed Methuen Publishing, 1982, 1985, 1986. 208 pp. A large volume of region-by-region description. Brief but well-written text and a wealth of breathtaking color photos.

——*North Island* (Mobil New Zealand Travel Guide). Fifth rev. ed. Reed Methuen, 1986, 326 pp.

——*South Island* (Mobil New Zealand Travel Guide). Fourth ed. Reed Methuen, 1986. 422 pp. Long, narrow, and heavy, but packed with useful information. The best on-the-road guides.

Shell Road Maps of New Zealand. Shell Oil New Zealand Limited, 1986. 57 pp. Indispensable and complete book of road and city maps. Sold only at Shell service stations in New Zealand.

Articles

Jordan, Robert P. "New Zealand: The Last Utopia?" *National Geographic Magazine,* May 1987, pp. 654-682. An insightful introduction to the people of New Zealand.

Index

THE KIWI LOG
To Remember the Good Times . . .

Use the handy forms in this section to record the practical information and the memorable events of each day of your trip. This will provide a useful and enjoyable memento that will help you relive your New Zealand adventure for years to come. And it will give you something to do in the campground after dinner.

KIWI LOG

TRIP DAY: DATE:

FROM: ODO:

TO: ODO:

WEATHER: KM TRAVELED:

PHOTOS TAKEN:	EXPENSES:
	FUEL:
	CAMP:
	GROCERIES:
	RESTAURANT:
	OTHER FEES:
	TOTAL EXPENSES:

HIGHLIGHTS & OBSERVATIONS:

KIWI LOG

TRIP DAY: _____   DATE: _____

FROM: _____   ODO: _____

TO: _____   ODO: _____

WEATHER: _____   KM TRAVELED: _____

PHOTOS TAKEN:	EXPENSES:
	FUEL:
	CAMP:
	GROCERIES:
	RESTAURANT:
	OTHER FEES:
	TOTAL EXPENSES:

HIGHLIGHTS & OBSERVATIONS: _____

_____

_____

_____

_____

_____

KIWI LOG

TRIP DAY: DATE:

FROM: ODO:

TO: ODO:

WEATHER: KM TRAVELED:

PHOTOS TAKEN:	EXPENSES:
	FUEL:
	CAMP:
	GROCERIES:
	RESTAURANT:
	OTHER FEES:
	TOTAL EXPENSES:

HIGHLIGHTS & OBSERVATIONS:

KIWI LOG

TRIP DAY: _____ DATE: _____

FROM: _____ ODO: _____

TO: _____ ODO: _____

WEATHER: _____ KM TRAVELED: _____

PHOTOS TAKEN:	EXPENSES:
	FUEL:
	CAMP:
	GROCERIES:
	RESTAURANT:
	OTHER FEES:
	TOTAL EXPENSES:

HIGHLIGHTS & OBSERVATIONS:

_____

_____

_____

_____

_____

_____

KIWI LOG

TRIP DAY: DATE:

FROM: ODO:

TO: ODO:

WEATHER: KM TRAVELED:

PHOTOS TAKEN: EXPENSES:

FUEL:

CAMP:

GROCERIES:

RESTAURANT:

OTHER FEES:

TOTAL EXPENSES:

HIGHLIGHTS & OBSERVATIONS:

KIWI LOG

TRIP DAY:	DATE:
FROM:	ODO:
TO:	ODO:
WEATHER:	KM TRAVELED:

PHOTOS TAKEN:	EXPENSES:
	FUEL:
	CAMP:
	GROCERIES:
	RESTAURANT:
	OTHER FEES:
	TOTAL EXPENSES:

HIGHLIGHTS & OBSERVATIONS:

Printed in the United Kingdom
by Lightning Source UK Ltd.
100906UKS00001B/540